SCARS ON THE SOUL

DEEPALI SEKHRI

Made with ♥ on the Notion Press Platform
www.notionpress.com

To

family

and

friends

Contents

Foreword

Scars on the Soul" is a collection of poetry that delves into the human experience, exploring the raw emotions and lasting impressions that life leaves upon our souls. This thought-provoking poetry book by Deepali Sekhri features introspective verses that resonate with readers on a profound level. The striking cover artwork, featuring a minimalist sketch of a figure with flowers blooming from within, perfectly captures the book's theme of growth through adversity. Each poem serves as a mirror to our own experiences, reflecting the beautiful complexity of healing and transformation. This collection is perfect for poetry enthusiasts who appreciate authentic emotional expression and artistic storytelling through verse. The book offers a meaningful journey through various emotional landscapes, making it an ideal addition to any contemporary poetry collection.The book will walk you through the deepest of emotions, the soulful thoughts and the everchanging world around us.

Preface

CONTENTS

Acknowledgements

For the Love

You carry in your heart

Hate can never be a choice.

Prologue

We have the growth power within

that's how

Beauty introduces

itself to the world

through us

Nature belongs to

out and within.

The destruction,

incarnation & regeneration

of the newness

has an ingrown seed

in the depth

of our conciousness.

1. HEALING

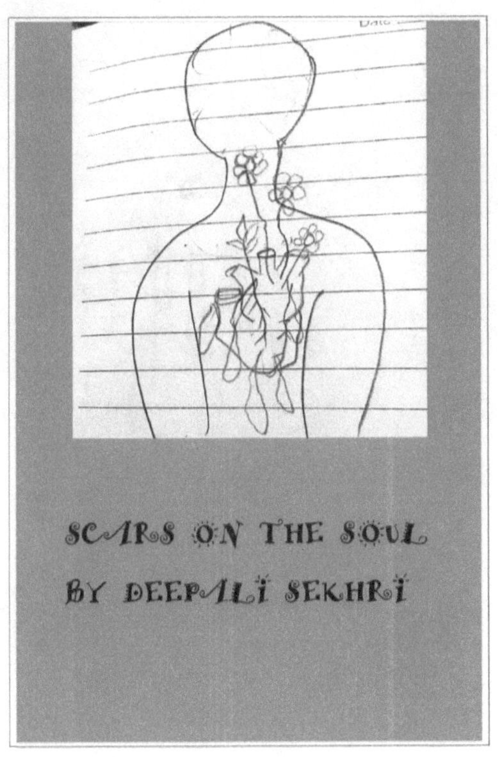

HEALING

TIME
Time is taking time
and I am afraid to pass through it
like sand particles.
- the body

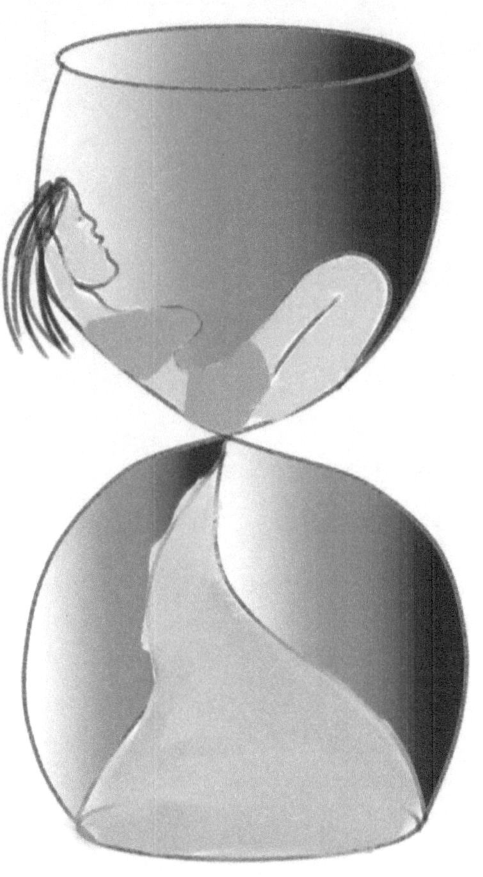

SEEDS OF LOVE

Out of all the homes
I have built all my life
in the hearts of people
I met .
The home I built in yours was made with strongest bricks.
Out of all the seeds of love
I sowed in different hearts
I wish the seed I sow in you
grow as a beautiful tree with roots
deep into your soul
giving flowers time to time
to nurture the peace in you to tell you ,
the falling leaves belongs to me
like the broken you
is ought to come for me
and the branches of this tree may give you the warmness
and the flowers remind you the fragrance of my love.

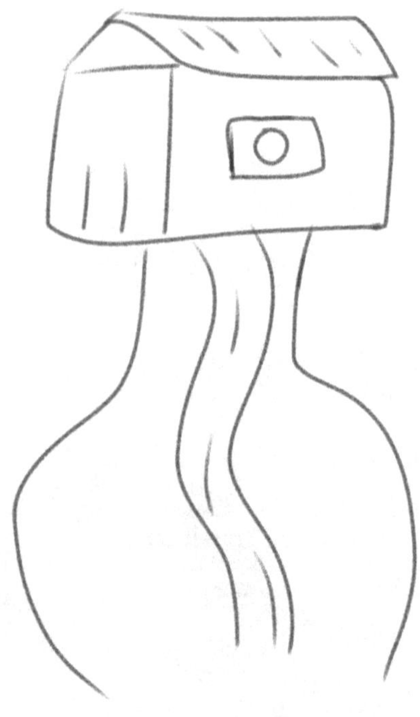

HEAL YOURSELF

Where ever you are in the process of healing just give yourself love and attention you seek from others . Just move the mountains for your own those you were ready to move for your loved ones . Lets wait for the sun to come out and shine exclusively for you and let your eyes meet the rays of hope after a while . Let the moon wait for you to end the dark night and send the time of dawn to you for your prayers. Let all the beauty in you to come out and blossom with beautiful flowers today . Let the day take you to a start over and give you the courage to carry your scars to your mirror to see them as rewards for the uninvited sufferings. Let all the butterflies in your stomach spread their wings to get to know life again . Let the water and blood in you , go, follow the rain. If you feel like crying for the one last time , cry. Let the river run. Nobody can fulfill your desire of feeling loved or the desire of feeling wanted , only you can . Also , you can't force the process of healing you are into . The love you give to yourself is the love you allow to receive . The love you foster within, for 'your own' is the love you radiate. Self love is the supreme form of love , it makes you independent because you stop seeking love from outside. Loving yourself entirely makes you accepting others selflessly . The more you love ,the more it radiates and with time it cascades into hearts . You build more heart to heart connections that stays beyond life times. Just remember you are required to give yourself the love you are seeking from others . you are responsible for the way they address you by treating yourself in ways accepted by you . You are going to supervise them with the love you deserve. You are accountable for every time you degrade yourself. Never disgrace yourself in front of people . its perfectly okay to crtically analyse but the thin line distinction between betterment and bitterness is always there.

-The love you foster

Is the love that radiates around you .

HOMES

Sometimes someone's heart sounds like another home to you . It's a soul to soul talk. You feel correlated to them and you genuinely want it to last longer and on a dark day, you watch them leaving you. You have lost them. The thing is you can stay at many places and not every home belongs to you . You can't really spend your whole life at a single place likewise the homes we built in each others heart sometimes may not be for our forever accommodation. Throughout our life odyssey, we move to different places , different homes . Sometimes we spend years and sometimes we are there for a day or a month and at times we think a heart is our permanent residence but with time, we have to leave from our hometown too. Before you find your destination that gives you internal satisfaction you may have many stopping points And it's perfectly ok to be lost sometimes , to feel empty inside until you bring serenity with chaos outside . Its better to understand that you have to say alot of goodbyes before you are finally ready to welcome what you actually need . Life never stops because somebody is not walking on the same path with you anymore we have to fathom the fact that nobody can stay forever. Wishing them happiness from distance have more meaning than bringing them a lifetime misery . Where you understand moving on without carrying the baggage of guilt is more important than staying and always blaming .

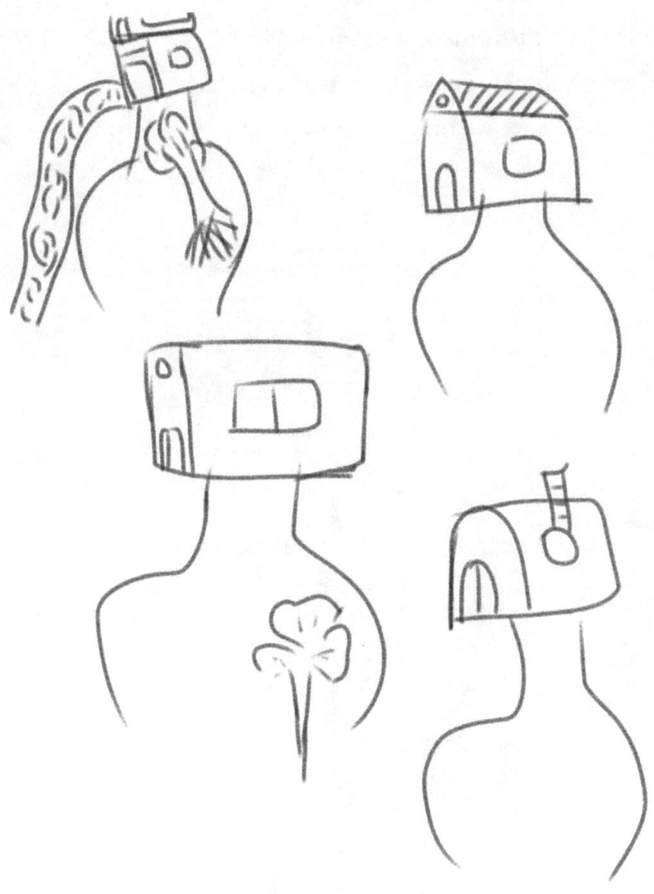

HEART AND TEARS

How Time turns memories into ashes
Ashes, we don't want to keep at home
Also, that ashes we don't want to pour
-Heart and Tears

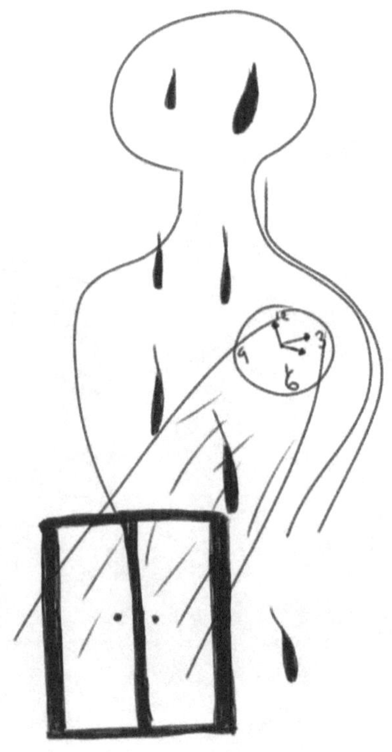

TIME

Time heals wounds
But can't teach you
How to unlove.

FREE
Isn't it amazing
To finally realize
You are not bound to hold ?

THE MOON

The moon says

I am able to shine in darkness

because I had the sun got my back.

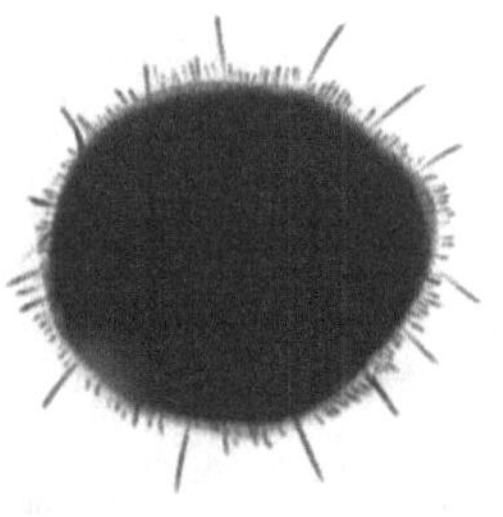

The moon says

your flaws are divine

RAINBOWS

You can't create your value
In the eyes of someone
Who is colorblind
To the rainbow in you .

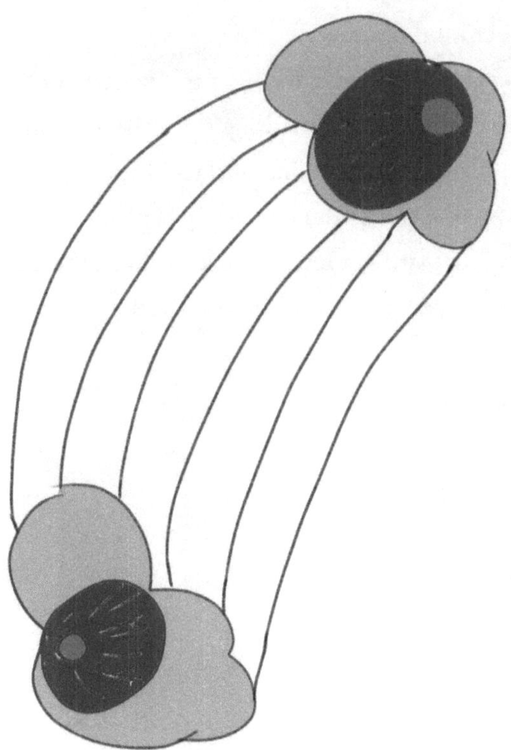

SHE

She dances in the rain

And cry in the pain

Rain, she escaped from

Drainage, she can't be saved from .

She sings with smile

And be loud when she talks

She was her kind of universe

The glitter in her eyes give the light to the galaxies

and the tornadoes were something she walks with , in her hair

her smile witness the sparkling of stars in the sky

and the way she carries the fire within capable

of burning the dark shadows of demons from the past behind

.

VINTAGE

Our ancestors born us modern build us palaces moved countries to find us homes,culture, nature and power. Our men depicted eminence courage to transform lifes and the women carried the burden of the world on their heads . They sustained and cycled the beautiful journey of life unravelled the language ancients speak. They signed our way to future. They laid skeletons to survive the humans race and showered the experience to mature us. to not mistake the human and its potential.

-Vintage

SELF LOVE

Self love is like a bridge that helps you build strong relationship with others.Self Love is the only aid we need.Its the only source of healing our soul to the core. "The person who love himself in all right ways will always recognize when people try to love him in wrong ways".On the journey of experiencing true love one knows original love don't come from seeking attention from others infact it flows naturally and effortlessly. If you feel sufferings in love save yourself from the garbage that people serve you in the name of love and make you sick.You can fight physical symptoms but mental symtoms are the real war.No matter how hard the fight is self love is the ship that will sail you away.It acts lika a bandage to your aching heart. Like a cure to damaged souls . It is like an antidote that neutrilize the sharpest edges of time.,Self love starts with self awareness more than that with self acceptance.While self awareness is the tool to build strong relationship with yourself , acceptance is embracing the dark part of it. Its like telling yourself that you need to master the art of being youself in your true sense.Its like surrendering to the beauty of love. "The one who knows the power of freedom is the one who knows how to free others." Self love is an ocean of love, acceptance , abundance of care.Its like sailing into the truthfulness of your being.

ENDURANCE AND BEYOND

Losing every hope on myself

After walking down on the edge of extreme

After enduring intense pain and regular heartbreaks

After getting exploited for my humbleness and good heart .

I still choose love over hate.

I still choose light over darkness.

I still choose scars over fake ointment.

HOPE

She was searching HOPE in you

Discovering it sprouted

Somewhere within the cracks of her broken heart .

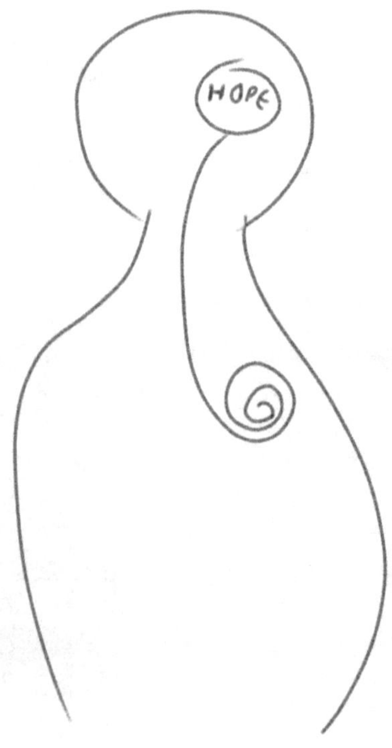

INEVITABLE CHANGE

Never fear the gradual changes life brings in you. Never fear the healing and time your heart takes to feel again . Never be afraid to start over from something you thought would stay but left without any explanations and deadlines or warnings . Never move in a way people want you to or Never try their way of healing . Yours is unique in your own . Slow progress in healing is the best method to feel and love again when a sudden heartbreak shallow your within . Believe the faith God have put in you for his ways . Walk and fathom every loop hole , remove the limitations in your way . He will surely exceed your expectations and not randomly but gradually you will know that you have been healed . You have always been guiding even when you thought of being cursed , actually it was a blessing in disguise . He is not going to come down on earth to tell you and calm you but there are angels called family and friends , they are present throughout the bad days and the good ones too . Sometimes God distance us from people and things , not serving our purpose in life . Some people are taken away from us because they didn't deserve a good heart like us . Some people need to leave for our good and even we are not good for certain people . Not every person is made to stay in our life . Some are just passengers walking by and we keep on dropping the fellowbeings in our way to destination but still we feel sad , we hold on the pain for so long that we forget the mystery is written by Supreme creator and he knows the best in our story . He sees the bigger picture , he knows our journey . We just need to be moderate and surviving throughout our healing process . Feeling low key and sad is a part of our life moments. So it's perfectly ok . But your heart It should keep beating . It should keep working in a way we feel alive even with emotional encounters . Believe the faith your god have in you and your becoming.

CURE

You are the medicine
I need to heal my soul with

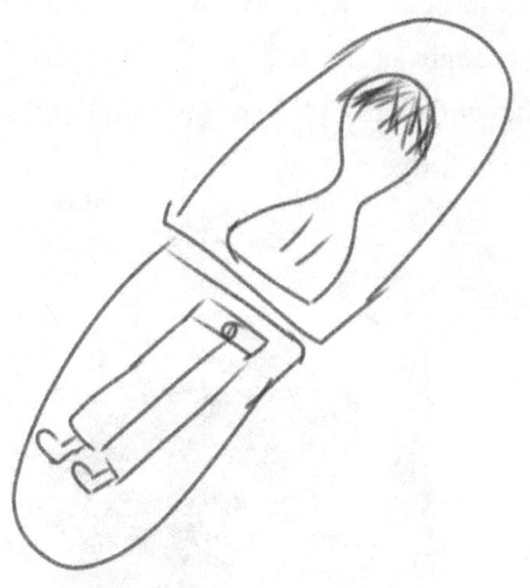

MUSEUM

My heart is a museum

For all the dead feelings

To keep feeling

hence the old love is never died

It breathes , it resides ,

In darkness or in light

Or with the thought of never arise

Forever is the word but YOU are immortal and safe here in

the home I built for you .

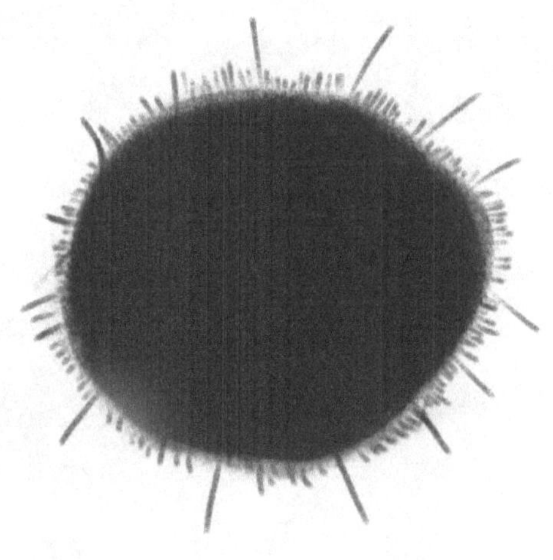

MOVE ON

You don't move on from people
you spiritually outgrow
them including yourself.

SELF REALISATION

Your pain ,sadness, weaknesses everything in this world that dishearten you, has a point of saturation where you need to find your own way back home . Where you need to stand up against the person you have just made , to look straight into darkness and find light out of it . Every bad chapter of life must have some good lessons . Everytime your mind torture you for the actions of others you need to remind yourself that you are a happy soul . That no matter who was or is at fault . You don't deserve this pain . You should not hold on to this pain as the pain can not belong to someone who is innocent . The point is to rescue yourself from the wandering sufferings , from pain that can never define you . Let healing come to you. Let extra ordinary magic of revival and growth embrace you from within . Let your self love prevail from the cheap love that this world is serving you with . Let you believe in the magic of changing your perspective towards the situation you have been dealing for so long but haven't planned any rescue yet . That you need to be feeling love from within , to be a better human who feels and breathe freshness . That I don't know who deserves this pain but definitely , I am not the one who is made to be the victim of others ungrateful , inattentive actions towards life . The strength lies in letting go of everything that doesn't belong to you including the details of the event that just happened , that you are trapped in right now . The growth lies in understanding and accepting your past wholly and holding on to your truth . No matter how long you have walked alone , no matter how much of the pain you have endured alone , you still have that courage to stand up , you have that zeal to fight back again with the same power . You still have that in you. The lion is always a lion even if it stays in a group of sheep for long . Go hunt your opportunities . Go run for your life . Go find your happiness . Go live , before you die.

UNCERTAIN DAYS

The days when you are in total uncertainy that you end up questioning everything around you including yourself . The days when you sit and critically analyse life . when you are at your extreme unfortunaty and even ready to give up . You feel like walking with no one behind and above you , you are just there pondering & questioning every bad thing, are the days of your making .These are the days when Universe is trying to whisper the integrity and chaos in your ears at the same time . You find yourself in the middle of nowhere and that's from somewhere you need to restart . These days you spend working endlessly and hours of your nights go by, to stand against the similarities and eventually you learn smirking with the odds . Remember you are always doing it right when you are at your utmost fragility . Your days of uncertainties are the power pack . These days drink you into one shot and puke the impossibilities out of you . Remember confusion lead you to certainty and it may be not be "the right" you were searching for but somehow GOD is helping you find a light through this hell , he is guiding you on your way to excellence and remark .

2. LOVE AND HEARTBREAK

LOVE AND HEARTBREAK

FEAR

Fear looks like

A tree losing its roots

A flower that refuses to blossom

A monsoon promising not to shower rain again

A night without your memories

A morning without a new beginning

An ending without a promise to begin.

A natural unknown death

A learning without a new trail

Fear looks like – our fate

DRINK THE TEARS

I will drink all the tears I had shed for you.

I will bundle up all the hurt and let it float in ocean.

I will sail through every last drop of it to make sure

its easy to swim now that you are no more in me .

I don't want to water the seeds of your ignorance in me.

I don't want your love running into my veins anymore .

I don't want myself chasing the same sky under which

I saw the sun rising with you.

I am no more in love with our impossibilities.

I am going bury our story somewhere deeper into earth's chest

so that no one can find it . Not even me .

I am always into resistance of not connecting

the dots of our love like beautiful mess of stars.

I am content watching you and

your particles in me disappearing into the dark abyss.

I don't fear the brittleness anymore.

I wear my thick skin like an armour

to calm the external combat .

I won't bargain that piece of my heart

thats been brutally broken by you.

For today I will drink all the tears I had shed for you.

PAIN & REGRETS

Just give me a knife

I want to give exactly

What hurts

when you go far

Let me rip my heart apart.

Let me cut the eyes as they can't see you going too far.

Let me cut my veins , the muscles that could not hold you enough to not let you go .

– pain and regrets.

BOREHOLE

I have dug a borehole into my soul
Where I 'll treasure you with
Each and every beat of my heart.

WARMTH

I am feeling the warmth of your breath within me
Maybe it's your heart beating inside.

• 42 •

SILENCE IN BREATHE

From the silence of my heart

Till I cease to suspire

You are in it till I am finally dead.

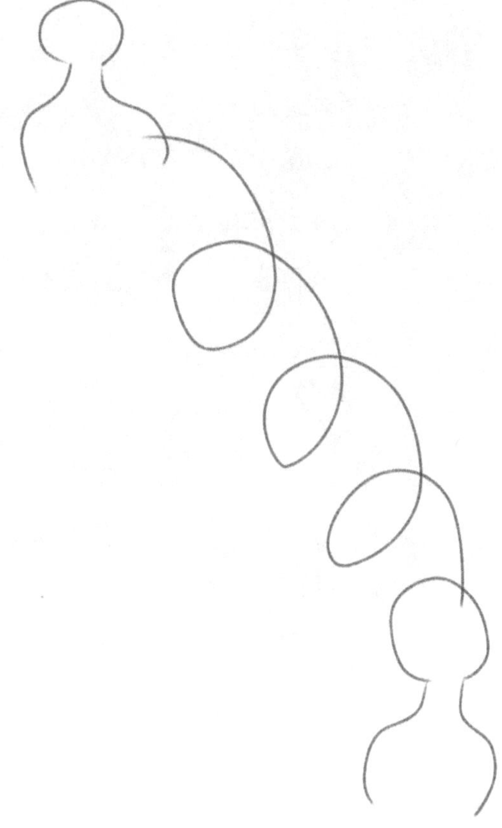

SILENT

I am turning on

To the silence of the sea .

And you are the reason

I am silent in me .

UNAIDED SCAR

You have left a hole in my heart
Unaided and uncensored .

HEAVENS

The heavens are weeping today

As we are falling apart

Like the stars from the sky.

I SAW HER
I saw her
Sobbing for people
Who don't care about her smile .
I saw her
Living in darkness
Due to people, blocking all the light.
I saw her
Fragile heart
Waiting for an elf
To awaken the strength In her veins.
I saw her
Marking breakdowns
Because nobody cared to pick up her broken pieces.
I saw her Fighting
Alone with storms
And saving her throne .
I saw her as a queen
Who had been offered thorns
Wrapped up with hopeful roses.
I saw her .

BROKEN HEARTS

Broken people have seen their heart ripped apart inch by inch feeling by feeling. Its like innocence leaving your home crashing every bit of hope into nothingness. Turning hope into phoenix. People fold their hands to pray they fold their body from head to knees for peace. Peace that has left them in dark heavy pain in heart head exploding with thoughts everything's dead but that light that saves them lil light that guides them stay alive.

DARKNESS

You are that darkness

With you even my shadow refuse to exist .

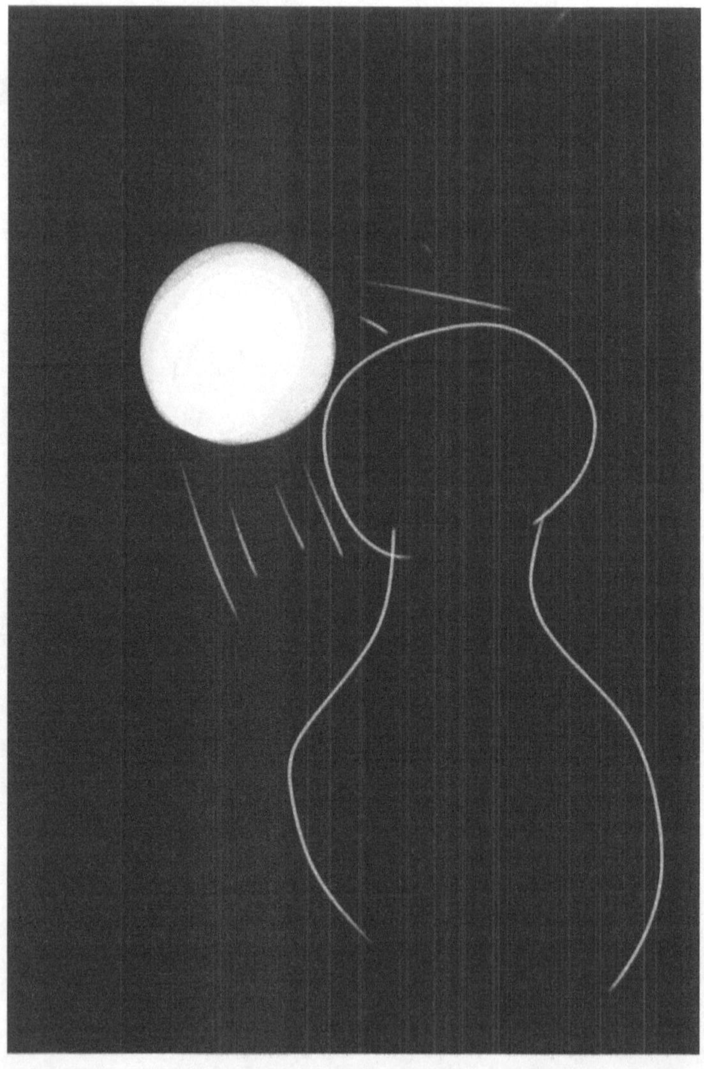

CHEAP LOVE

Cheap love is everywhere .you see lot of people today loving you in all cheap ways and the thing is you don't have to struggle for it . You don't have to put your money and heart into buying it bc people out there serving this kinda love with their alluring mind games wrapped up with broken promises and fake personalities. It's available 24 ×7 in the market like you need to bear 0% risk to buy it and with no expectations of returns. It's more like a legal scam and always a game where you will surely lose all your players.

ROTTEN

All the flower seeds

I planted inside me

Grew up and now they all rotten

Because I fed it with leaking blood

When I was supposed to water it .

OXYGEN

You are more like fresh air to me
I still breathe you
To oxygenate my blood .

POSSESSED LOVE

I don't know how to feel love. I have never been loved without pain . Everytime I used to experience love on skin. I have been told of I had to breathe , I had to feel love to those greedy eyes. I was told pain and love need to co exist . I don't know how to love without giving pain . I was taught being wild and heinous when it comes to show my love. For me it was pretty normal to love someone with lots of bruises and scars. That's how I have told if they love you somedays they will rule over you too and you have admit it . You have to be ok being processed and achieved .

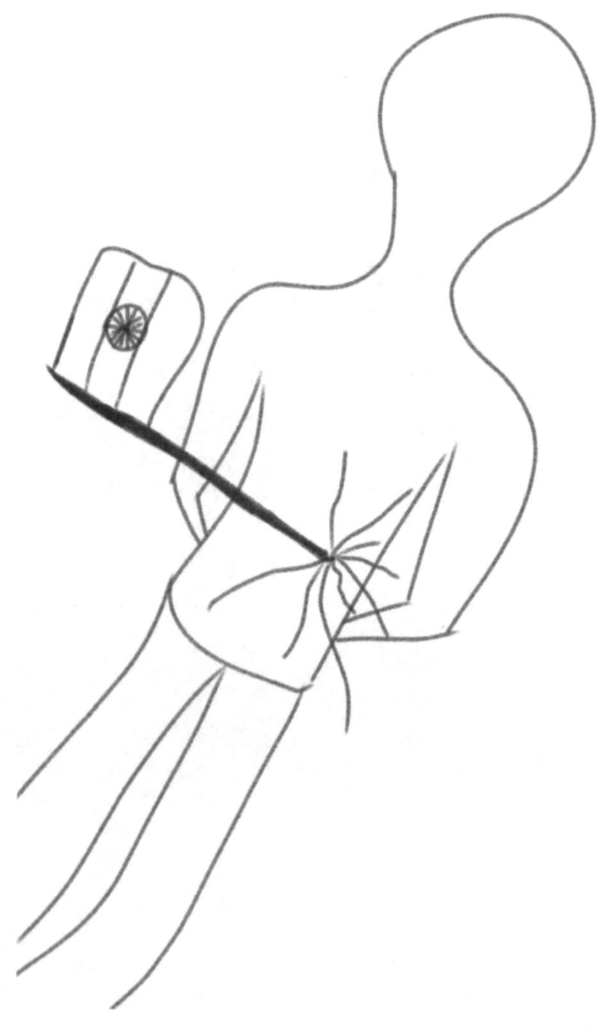

LOVE APART

I love you so much
That If I couldn't make you smile
I will end up crying with you .

FLAMES OF LOVE
Don't ever let the pain
Come out of you as volcano
BC it leaves you agonized
with flames as remnants .

JUSTICE
We only suffer
when we take justice in our hands
Leave justice to GOD

DARE

I Dare you

To take me

Skin on skin .

raw , courageous and soulful .

ABANDONEMENT
And After years
He wrote in his letter to me
You were my safest home
But I abandoned you ,
giving heartbreaks .

INSECURITIES

I have my people
replacing me like
they are changing clothes
-roots to my insecurities

FEEL

I feel you beneath my skin
When I feel memories and pain .

• 65 •

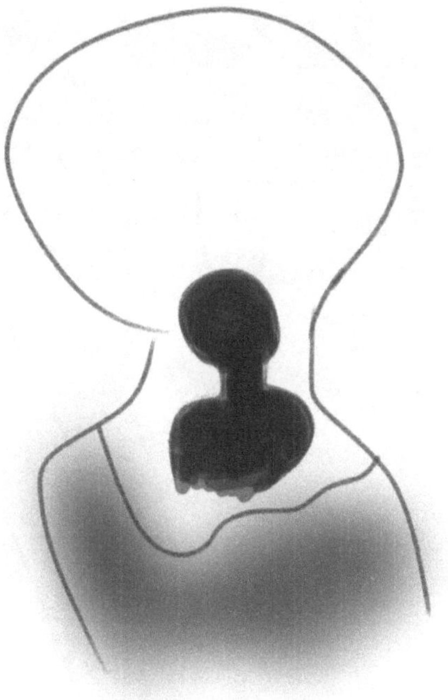

THIRSTY

Don't be too thirsty
For love
That you end up drinking
Every heart YOU meet

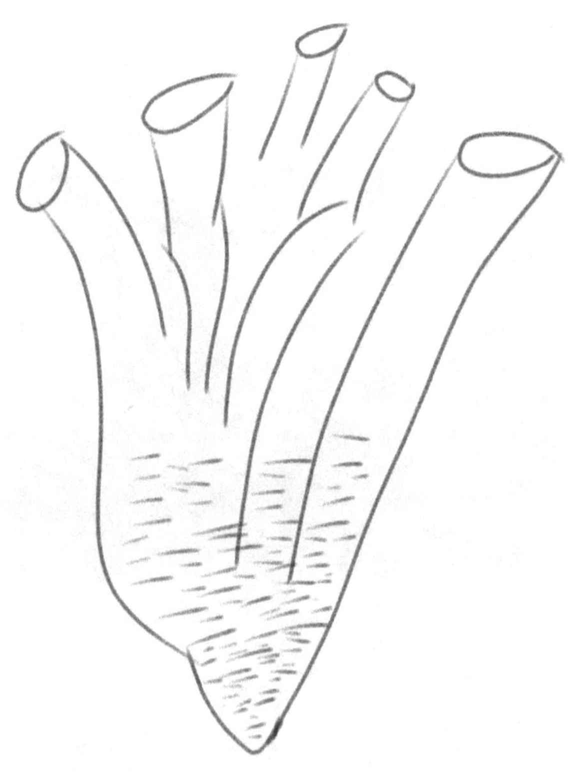

SHOWER OF LIGHT

CANVAS

Soak me in you

in a way a canvas

submerge the colours .

PROMISE
Whenever someone
promises me
Forever
I ask for an always

MYSTERY

I can't dead you .

I can't let you in .

You are a mystery I can't solve .

COME ON

Come on walking the road with me .

I pour you my heart

I ll bleed my veins .

For you , my love

I won't mind getting on my knees

I ll take you to the full moon

Come on the sky with me

We ll make a constellation

I ll take you to my universe

I ll give you some flowers

For you my love

I ll offer you some stars

Come on to the city with me

I ll take you to a long ride

We ll end up dancing in the rain

Shoving up madness with all our brain

We ll end up on a flight

I may promise to let you win in our fight

For you , my love

I ll let go beyond my skin

I ll tell you my childhood days and the stupidest of my life
trails

Come on the empty nights with me

I will shower your soul

Naked and whole

And make you feel bright

I ll buy you some jeans
So I can wear it , every fifteens
try your scent , to get high on your essence .
Come on .. on the track with me .
My love .

POUR THE HEART

I pour you my heart
You drink it in words .

ROAMING

Lets just roam
Out in the sky
Covering the whole universe
Let's just fly
Lets crave Moon as deity
And worship it's blemishing like stars
Conquering the quest
make it a rapture of glory .

BURNING HEARTS
You meet so many burning hearts
our whole life
With the only hope that someday
we ll meet somebody flaming
In the same sort of light .
With the same fight .

EMPTY

I would rather be empty and soulless
Than breathing life without you .

TUG OF WAR

You are letting other voices get louder in your head than the love your heart ever had for me. But you know, this tug of war will soon come to a conclusion. I know eventually love wil win although all the time love suffers more than it needed to . Maybe the end has been detected far ahead but a lot has been lost in the journey. Finally what exactly we get is indifference. The exact opposite of love.

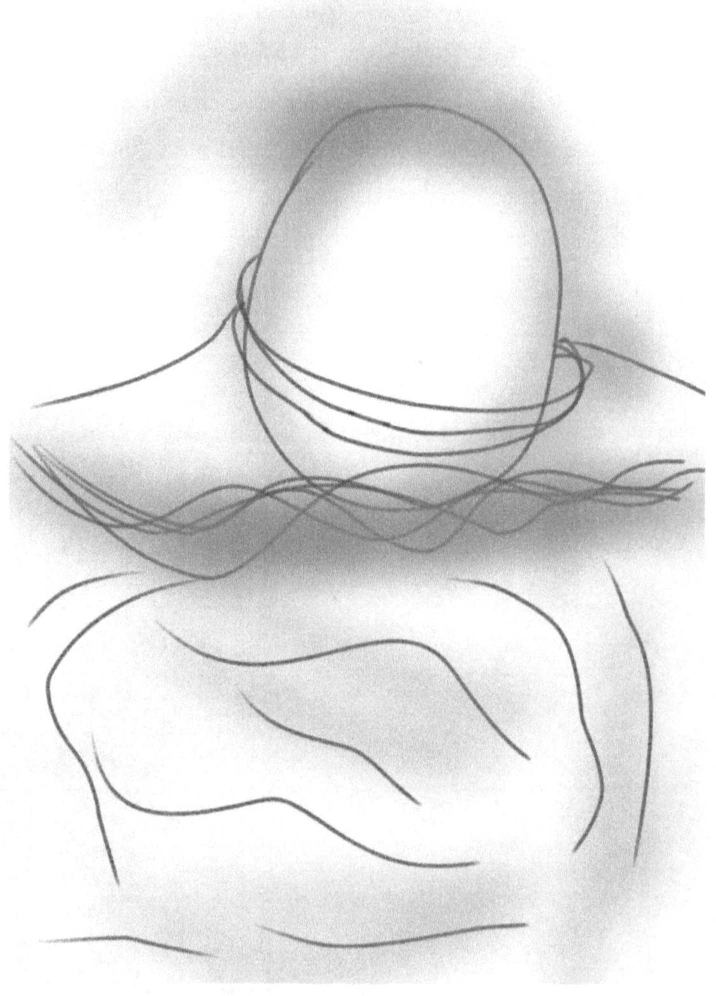

SCARS ON THE SOUL

OUR DREAMS

Our dreams are more like a teared tree in a snowbound area .

I can see a large abandoned area

Where I am waiting for you with our tree of dreams

HIDDEN

Stay hidden

Love will find you.

FEEL NOTHING
And one day all
we feel is nothing
but empty and shattered and lost.
Even within our heart,
our home we learn to be cold.

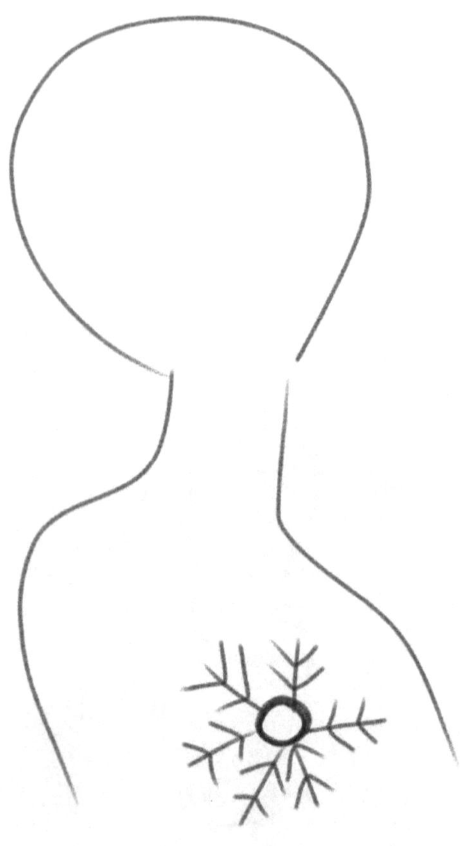

WEIGH OF MEMORIES

I weigh more

When I carry your memories with me

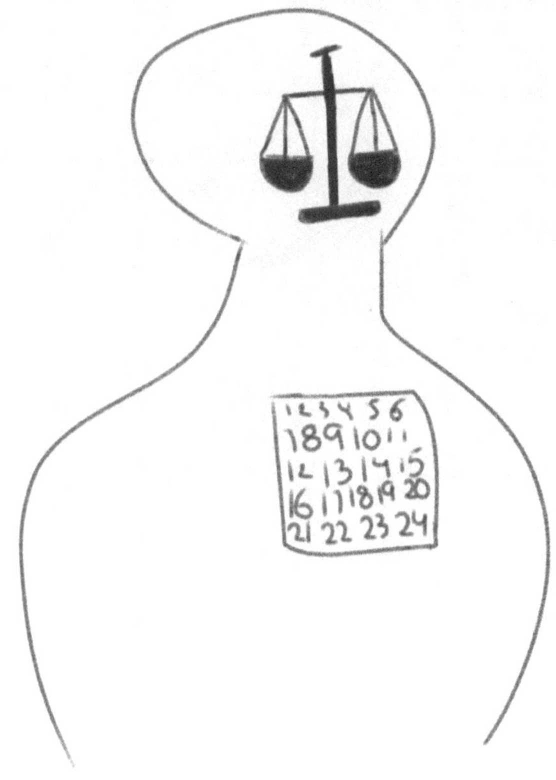

CRACKING OF HEART
Like an abandoned building
Witness the sound of cracking
I hear it coming
from the walls of my heart

- without you.

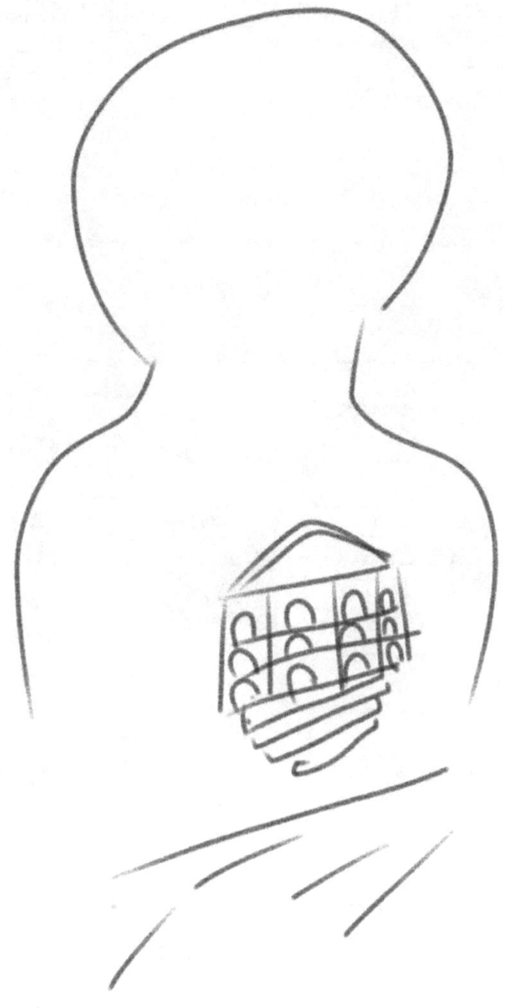

HEARTBREAK

Even the home built with the strongest bricks collapses

- heartbreak

YOU ARE YOUR OWN COMFORTER

GOOD PEOPLE

Good people. Somebody that give no judgements and love our inside out . Someone that look for the brighter side of ours and can build us wisdom of their soul . We crave their attention and always look for deep connections like this . We search for the good people and some people who take us with no changes , give us space and time for healing . Someone who can sit with us under the moon & looks for the shining stars and we don't hesitate pouring our heart for them . Someone as Good as their words and as transparent as their mind . A person who can take you as somebody as you are . Ready to burn the bridges of ego and envy between . We all in short just want to be found and appreciated. Someone who notice even the slightest change in our behavior or listening to our voice .

GOOD PEOPLE

Good heart for ourselves . Good heart tend to see the hope in us when we are resilient to it . Good hearts embraces the darkness we hold within and love us regardless of our sins. The internal flames of our soul feel ignited out of control , it all seems like casting a spell on me. When a good heart starts to read us we barely need to speak.

PILGRIM TO VULNERABILITIES

I am a pilgrim to my vulnerabilities

Travelled all my way to wrong things

To feel them on point , right .

I am a colourful spring ready to come up with all my highs

after autumn. Let all my leaves spread their wings to the roads

that lead to you .

I am no a saint , no a firefly

But I still feel like cheating gravity falling free In the sky for

you

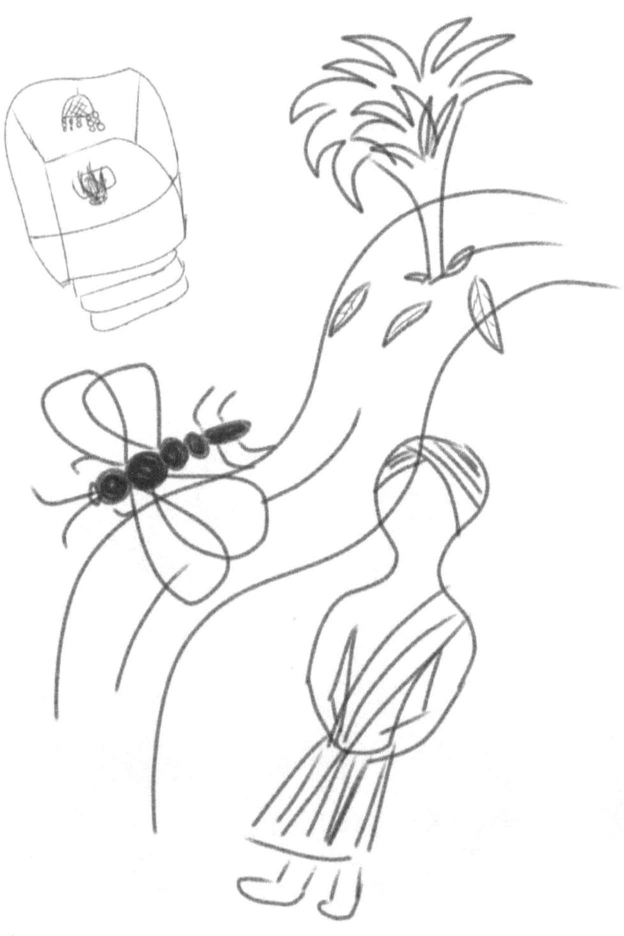

HOLLOW CAST

You served me with emptiness

In love

See I have made a hollow cast in my heart for all my feelings I had for you .

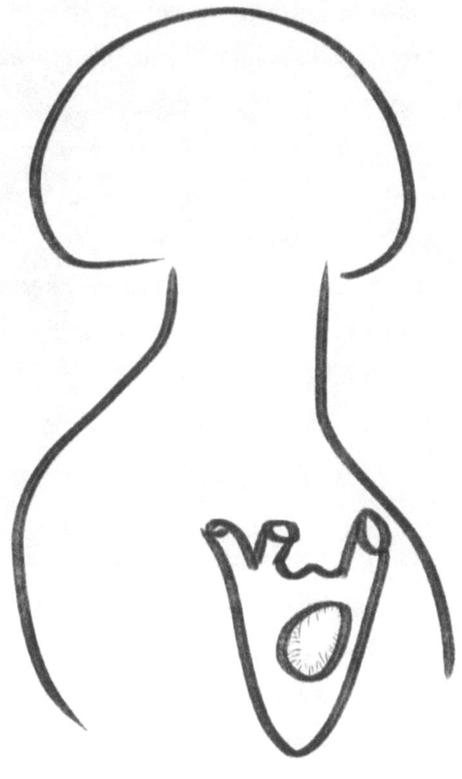

MAYBE

Maybe I understand you
Maybe I understand your words
Maybe I am in love with you
Maybe the world can't hear the chaotic thumbing of our heart
Maybe the silence prevail it all
Maybe the sky is not that impossible
Maybe the roads will always make desperate sense
Maybe the rainbows give us both a color
Maybe my poem knows what I ll never write to you
Maybe I stood there numb waiting for you
Maybe I wasn't supposed to do it all
Maybe your eyes tell me the details of your heart
Maybe the heart had a hollow cast of your buried emotions
Maybe I was bound to fall for you
Maybe you were never a stranger
Maybe the tree of my love never planted it's roots in your chest
Or maybe it's the possibilities of the my hopeful riot
Maybe innocence of your soul always made sense to me
Maybe you never tried to read my right
Maybe the letters i wrote to you were not meant to reach
Or maybe I should have kept it as a teach
Maybe the emptiness in words is sounding more loud
Maybe the thunder nights had all the clouds I cry for
Maybe you were meant to fade away
Or maybe to just stay a little bit more

Maybe I should have hugged you tighter
Maybe I should have not let the air cross by between the beats
of our mourning hearts
Maybe you were the fanatasy I wanted to believe on
Maybe the sky knows us both
I believe the god hears us both .

SEASONS OF LOVE

Even the coldest of the mountains melts
It's just a change of season that is needed .

LIKE A LEAF

Like a leaf

Finding its composure

I saw him

Running on the pavement

Tryin' to find rainbow of love .

INFINITE PEOPLE

There are infinite number of people in the world today and the infinites are looking for their kind of one in the crowd of infinites. We all are struggling , juggling hard to make our way back to home . Back to someone we can own. There are infinite possibilities of our kind of being. There are infinite type of love and care , maybe some of them we all seek . But have you ever wonder which one is you , which one you can call your own , which one make sense to you. Have you ever wonder that love has no boundaries it have no shape ,no form of its own. Love is all that we all need . Love is all we always want to breathe .but have you wondered why we all think we are in vain ? It won't even matter if we exist . Nothing in this world will make sense without the love . But love is something we are all searching , we are all longing for. So yes , love is the love when it comes to you . Love is true when it comes your way and try to sooth you . Love is someone making efforts to reach your soul . Always gazing and always their to adore . Love is someone calling you home as love is something you can't behold . Love is something that is windy , in the air crossing the bridges of ego and abandoning . Love is someone caring for you , in your darkest nights staying with you . Love is someone ready to move , moving mountains or the stars or the moon . I guess love is someone that comes to you when you are hoping or even not hoping it will always comes to you . Always

MAYBE

Maybe in our walk together

You have moved few steps ahead of me .

I don't blame you

Maybe I was so lost that

I didn't notice the road and footsteps or never stop following

the heart ..

Maybe I am left behind

Or maybe I have walked miles without you

I don't claim you

Maybe you were just the illusion of how it ' ll be

Maybe you were my hommie

Or maybe a stranger walking beside me

Maybe I could hear your silence

Or your wild words hit my heart

Maybe life is smashing us with fake success

Maybe sky is jealous from both of us .

Maybe our love is so mountain

Or maybe we both are allured by any saint .

Maybe the autumn is down the road

Maybe the winter is quite and more cold

Maybe we are supposed to breathe it out

Maybe it's all just a thought cloud

Maybe the footsteps were nothing

Maybe our heads were smithing

Maybe it was all in vain

Or maybe it's just because of rain .

Maybe my poem is meant to rhyme
Maybe time has done all the crime .
Maybe are just maybe .
A never ending riot .

WAR

Every breath without you
Feels like I am fighting a war
And losing against myself

GLORY

I cut my tongue short
For the glory of your word

PEOPLE

Some people meet you as a mystery

And die inside you as a mystery

For a mysterious reason

GRAVEYARD

I have dug a graveyard
For all my feelings for you
And promised myself to never
reopen it .

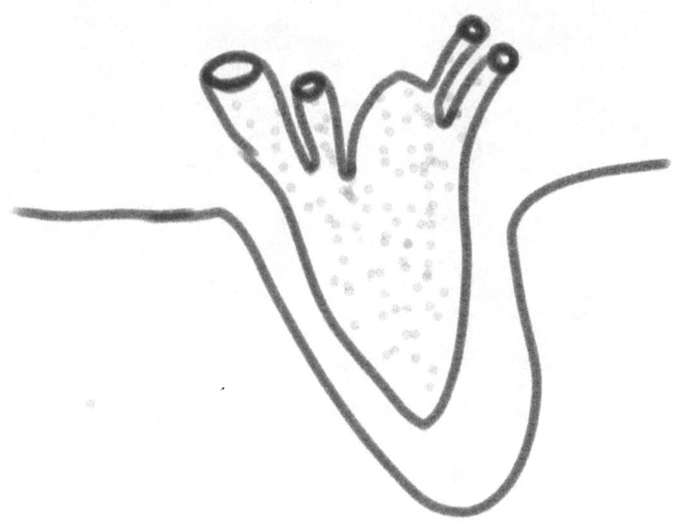

SOUR

My heart is souring

I don't cry

I suffocate.

ENOUGH

Enough of writing about thunderstorms

Or cactus instead of roses with thorns

Enough of bleeding and red-hot rains

Or knives deciphering unhealable wounds

Enough of writing about never ending times or tickling of the clock in nights

Enough of the colourless rainbows and black and white

Enough of sounds piercing the veins of mind or the bursting of the heart full of crimes .

Enough of fighting with demons or the poetry about the beauty of favourite human .

Enough of painting the tints of darkest dreams or use of vile , blunt tongue

Or starving for an unleashed beast

Enough of tarnishing the wildness through wild red cravings

Enough of writing about incredibly brutal revolutionary symphony

Or the lawless almighty deciding to numb our realisations .

I am all done with this . I am all done about fabric , artificiality or the functionality of the societal myths . I am all done with running mouths or the complexities of the harmonious generosity of humanity I am all done .

BITTER THAN POISON

Once it's over , move on

Don't get ruled by memories

They are bitter than poison

Poison kills you but memories eat your inside .

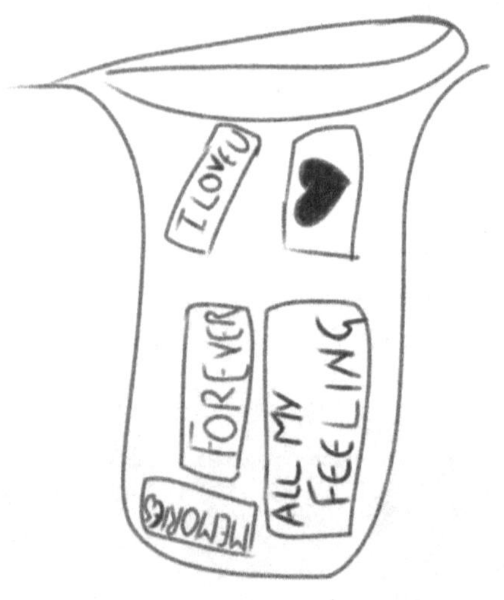

I LOVE U
FOREVER
ALL MY FEELING
MEMORIES

WORSHIP

I want to burn all thats
in me but worshiping you.

LOOKING IN LONGING

I looked for you till my eyes turned into tourmaline
Till whiteness turn into a moonstone
Till heart's hope turn into head's despair
I looked for you .

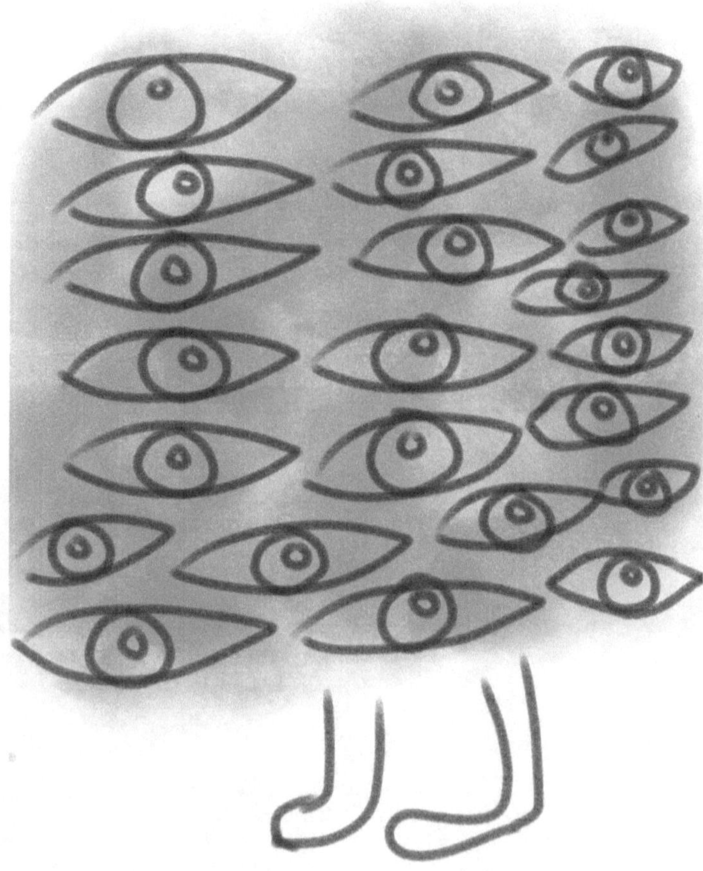

SWALLOW

Chew your words before spitting them out
See if you can swallow it with ease

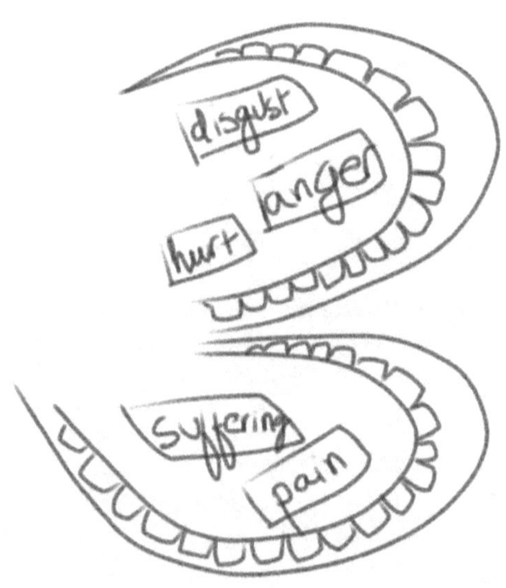

HUMANS

I experience humans differently
I I don't feel them the emotions
I experience vile impediments
Instead I see them passing by
Making judgement to each others existence
I just don't be bothered by human like "creatures"
they aren't themselves most of time
they are someone's emotions
someone's desires and the result of their own past
They tend to become people they hate
They behave like people who they hurt
They look like people who they desire
They inherent sickness from the people they love
That's how it is
they preserve the roots and kill the branches
they give away the fruits and cut the straights
They don't nurture they eat people s feelings
They don't cry they drink the tears instead
And water the soil and produce poison
They don't let live they become snakes
and don't hiss on bad they hiss on goodpeople
They feed on goodness and dunk the sins

GOLDEN

You are the gold of my life
As golden as the light of the moon
I find you in darkness
Shining bright in the night

MODERN LOVE

My lover is a sinner

And magician

I can't see him but feel

I stumble to get him in range

Modern love

COFFIN

I have made my body

A coffin of your memories

Buried and rotten for years

COFFIN OF MEMORIES

3. GROWTH

• 126 •

GROWTH

GROWTH

Growth is growing out of your shell .

We all have some expectations from us . And we all are trapped within our conflicts , our boundaries that never actually exist , some grown up watered enough ungrateful plants standing up on their terms while some on bigger terms than we are . Growing is all about that . Where you should just let it all go , forget who you were before , ready to stand at nothing , the point where you are empty enough to refill your senses , your mind with things that belongs to you . Growth stands with you at times when you learn standing up on your terms in life and understanding life on a bigger note . When you are ready to favour yourself with all the rights happening to your life . When you allow the higher standard adopt you. When you give up on all the wordy temptations and you can visualize the unusual . All the best imagined hurdles have fallen from grace in order to support your wisdom . When you are finally ready to overrule the forces of darkness and your flawed reality . Then growth comes to you , when you stand against everything that is not standing up enough for you .

LOVE DECEPTION

I am trying to move on without mourning

on the deaths of my previous lover

Oh !! how well I trade

My sanity for the love

I am recklessly walking on the dead's

How cruel is for a man to live beyond ashes

I am not your creepy regular person

That longs for you in the empty

I might sit on sadness and build concretes from my emotions

And may I just cut open the chest of earth to

look inside any traces of humanity to exist

As I dive deep into it and can't find no warmth,only coldness

I have curated the crime and started to live with it

Ready to hunt and eat the purity

How careless of a human I have become

to shred the heart and not keep an evidence

I have become the sins and came to world with its own reflection

Look what i am dressed as

Did You see a skeleton straight from the hell of love

Or a dog whose force fed the pain and made to survive..

IF PAIN IS THE ULTIMATE DESTINATION

You don't know what pain is

until you have pale eyes

a bursting headache

with swollen dry eyes

a soar throat

a shaking breathe

in a trembling body

and a heart unable to feel .

A place ,

Somewhere,

Tears have forgotten their way out of you

and you are left with a soul

which could not scream

it's pain loud,

just drinks it like a sip of poison.

If pain is the ultimate destination

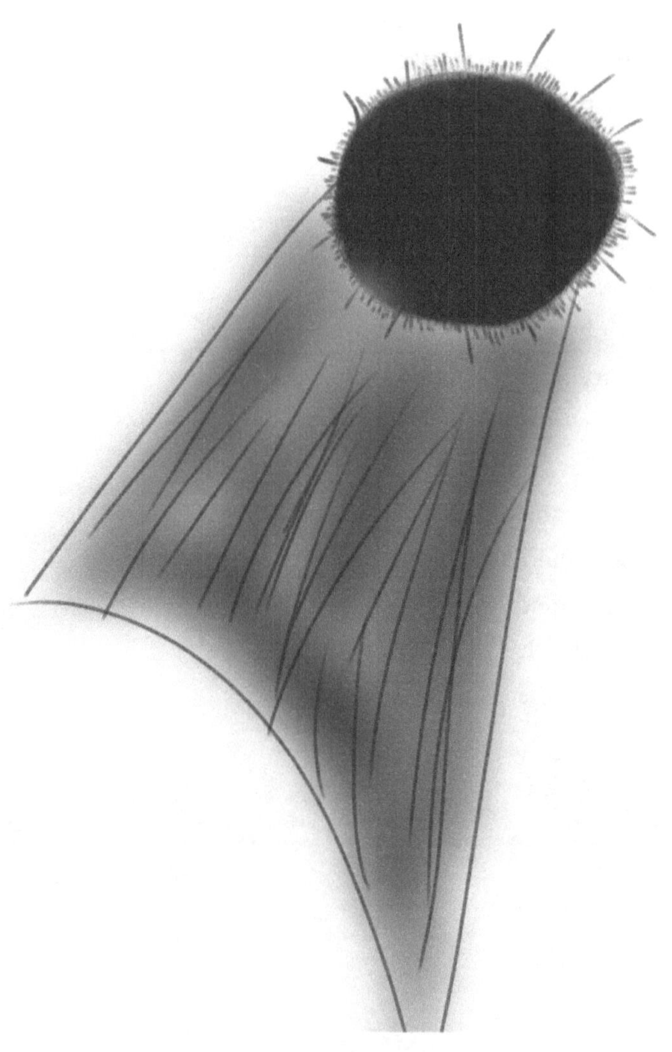

CHORDS

Now that I have

detached the chords

that used to connect us

I am at peace

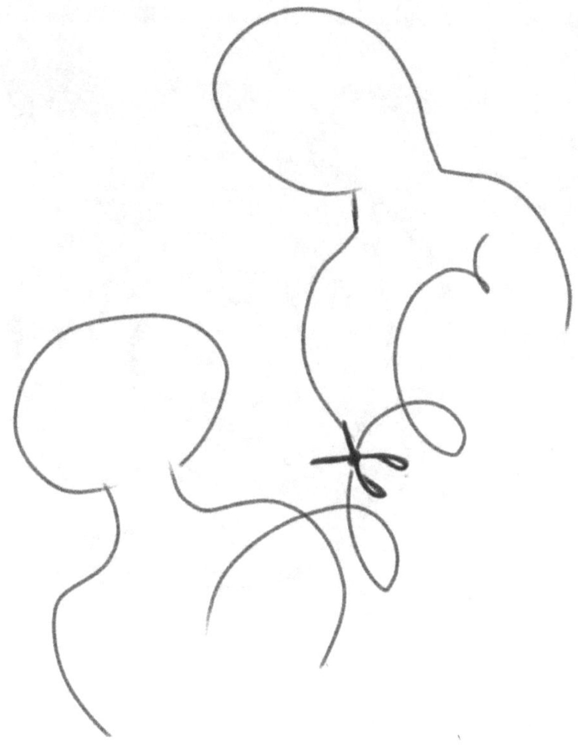

CIRCLES

People who go through hell
Burn someone's heaven
Circles

MASTERPIECE

Every eye is carrying a world in it.

A new and unique narrative of the world.

Our world is same but unique from others.

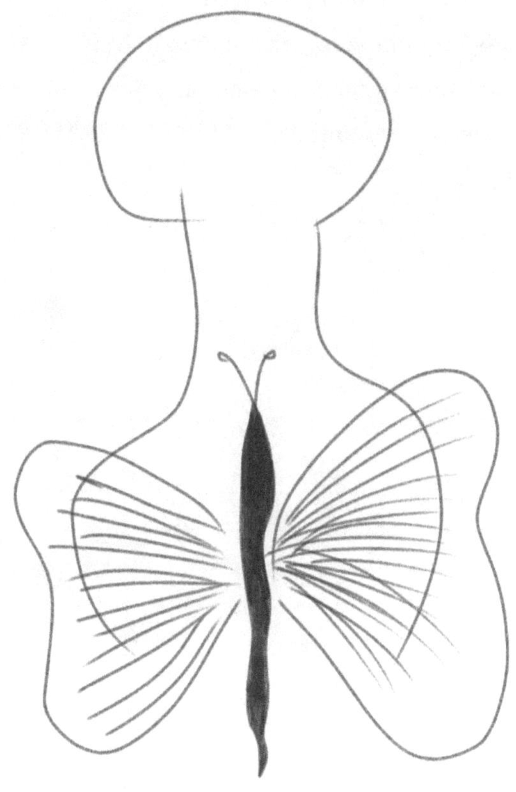

EAGLE EYED

I flew at the tip of hill and

Smashed myself into it so to destroy and recreate

I ate my own wings so for new to rise and bring me peace

I sang a song and hymned grief

I broke my hands, to remind myself that

the wounds I try to touch, are not here to feel

that pain is flames of roaring redemption

and gain is laced accommodation

-eagle eyed

BRIDGE OF TEARS
They named the bridge after me
And I kept time travelling
Screaming
save me, from me
might the night seems darker than it should be
And the stars have staired beeming straight into my eyes,
trying to find moon
But something in me keeps travelling back and
forth to you holding what we had
I carry the implants of our love in my existence
but I am afraid I don't get swamped away by it
I turn to sleep to release myself from being
puppet of our long lost love
and wake up in alternate universe
where us look like a possibility
and I don't have to make sense to reach out to you
and where I am not alone when I am with you
and we do the love that I dream of
That in my pain you are with me
but it isn't natural
You are one of them who stay when all is well
but leave when I desire your need
Your love might have came naturally to my trained mind
but it isn't real
It's all in vain
I hope they name it a bridge

Just a bridge ..
Not a bridge of tears
That connect you to me.
They named the bridge after me
And I kept time travelling
Screaming
save me, from me

PIECE OF PAPER

I am in two parts
like how we tore apart a piece of paper
for own self motive
without caring
for the natural role of it

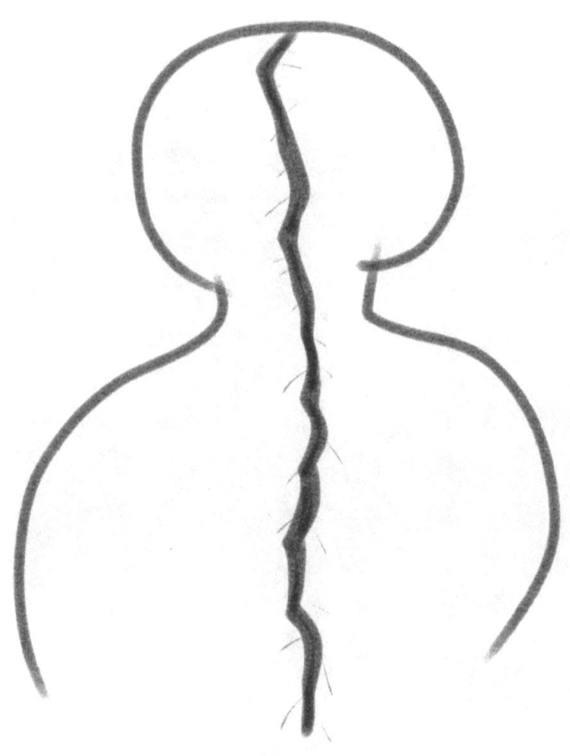

BETTER TO DIE
It's better to die and
Look at the world
From the place of refuge
O bloody river!!
I can see you dripping heavy
It's better to cry
And blur the vision of sky
From the red eyes
O lost dream !!
It's time to touch the heights
It's better to hive
For saving the crown
To name the castle of highs
O dear honey!!
My love might give you dive
It's better to be a knife
To cut and shred
Whatever comes in way
From the bottom till up at the top
O dead body !!
You reserve no place to hide
There is no god to human
Than it's own self motive
It's better to die …

LOVE

Look for me when I am not around

May be I am just a thought away

And when you miss me

Just hug the thought of us together

Maybe you ll feel the way

In a world of millions

We are just two for us

And if you ever lose the sight of me

How I look or what you see

Just turn your hands

And touch your eyelid

Like how we do when we bow

To GOD

In that prayer I am near

No matter how far but we are rear

When you close your eyes

You have my dream and

I am your lover and

If we are not together

We ll burn the world to ashes

- Love

SILENT
The body is aching
The heart burned and bursted into pieces ,
for the fire beside
chest I had ,
is now the graveyard of my feelings for you
and the body is the abandoned building witnessing the crime
,
the cries are the lullabies I sing myself to sleep at nights ,
the smile I wear all day is the skin I shed every night .
The loud loud thundering of clouds is the music
I listen to calm my demons .
And when a woman roar
You won't hear it
Because she is silent now .
- crushed enough

VERSE BY VERSE

I read poetry

One line at a time

Sip by sip

Breathe by breathe

I watch it touching my soul

And I let it consume myself

poetrygasm

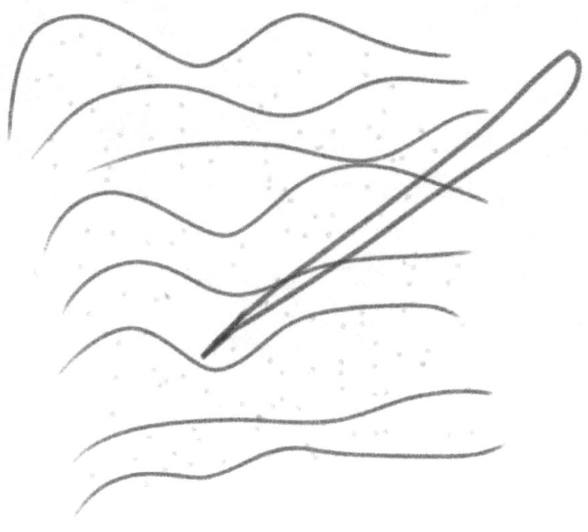

LIFE ISN'T ENOUGH

You and I are together
with million stories
to tell and life isn't enough

PERKS OF DISTANCE

All the noises around me
Tells how close you are to me
The louder / silent it gets
The emptier I feel without you
perks of distance

COLOURS

My room is full of colours

Colour of pain, love, hate and remake

• 146 •

OINTMENT

I need ointment
For my aching heart

MY HEART IS FULL

MEANT TO PART

It took me years to accept that

we were meant to part

I still contemplate your departure

My heart knows no answer to this misery

I only console it with tears, retrospection and love.

ENEMY

The enemy wants you to fall down and never get back
And God wants you to hit right against his spineless wish.

POWER OF A SOUL

These ordinary people do extraordinary

Every single time

They go save a life, feed a life

Build a home and

Sometimes when life draining slowly from their bodies

They might be born common but no one dies a common man

Every single soul is God's angel

And everyone is fight hard with the enemies to win a life

No wonder why I don't fear nothing at all

Even death doesn't scare me infact it enlightens

the idea of dying makes me laugh hard

on people's reactions

their imagination

their pain

Cause now I know

no pain is bigger than the resistance I have inside

I don't fear future

don't fear human

I just look at them

And Know God exist right there

Somewhere in all of us

-Power of a soul

WOUNDS

Until my wounds are addressed
I'll keep simmering the same blood.

LOOKING BACK

My heart succumb a little
When I look back and feel the years
I have lived without you

STILL

It hurts to remain still

DESTINY

Look at my destiny
You cant dead me
And I can't die …

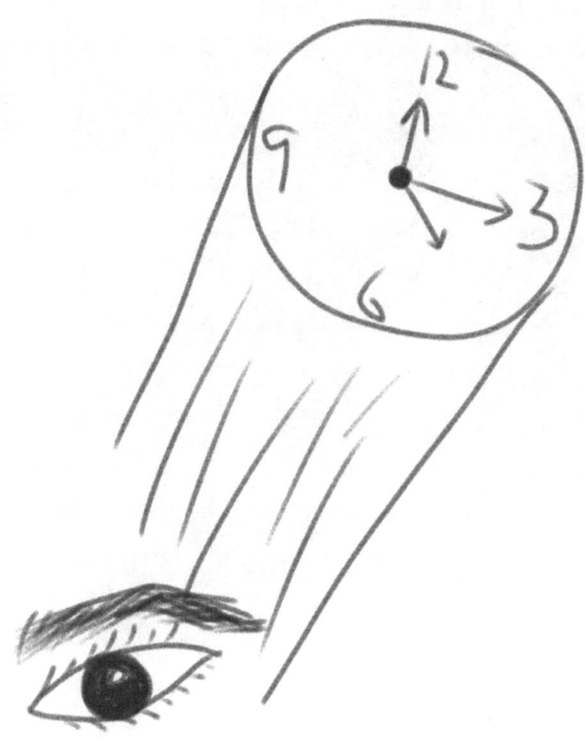

SLIP OF HANDS

If ever I slip from your hands

And you feel the distance between

Travel it

Sometimes I need you

Without having to explain

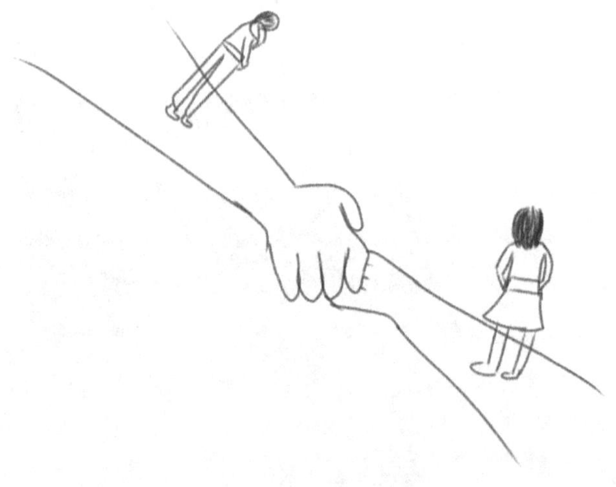

GROUNDED IN LOVE
And in love
People are reduced to ashes
You love your lover
So you don't quest
You just sit there and remember
Who you love and what you are
If love is your gut and heart
You consume ache like it's a treat
grounded in love

ON THE VERGE

Couldn't decide if I am losing it all

Or on the verge of gaining myself

LET GO

I have walked miles after you
Still feel like I ve never moved on
–let go

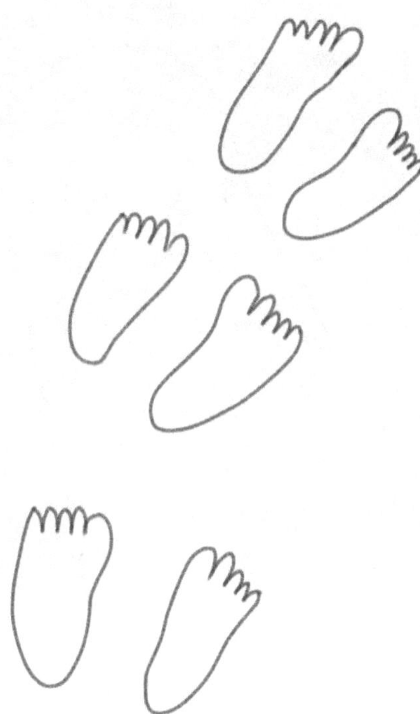

LET GO

I have walked miles after you
Still feel like I ve never moved on
–let go

LIGHT

If my words hit you In dark

Mind it they are complimenting your soul to light .

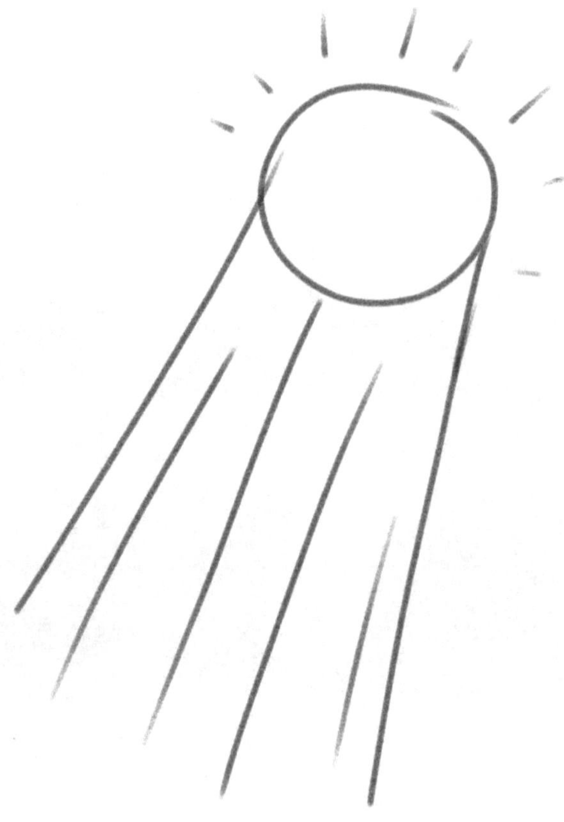

MOVED APART

I moved from
Heart to heart
Place to place
Without you.

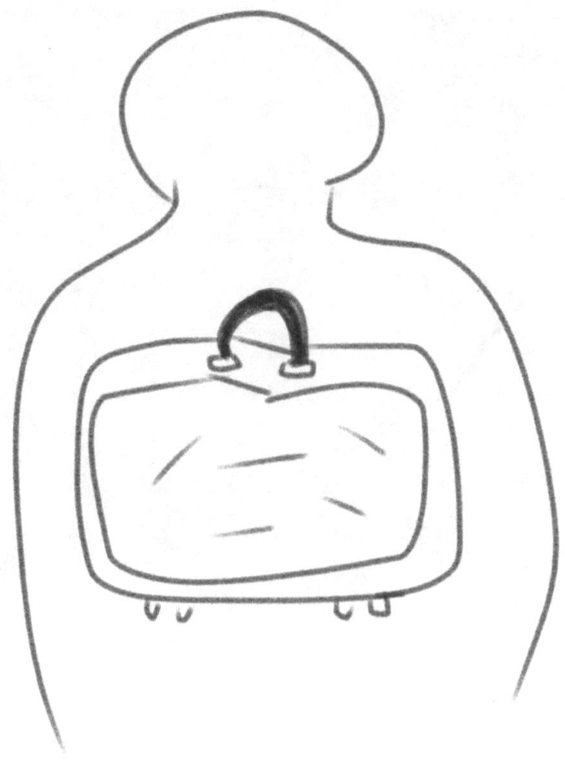

THE GRIEF

Longing for you
Is like
Sitting besides dead's
In the graveyard
And loath onto
The pain , the grief
Of losing you
-for forever

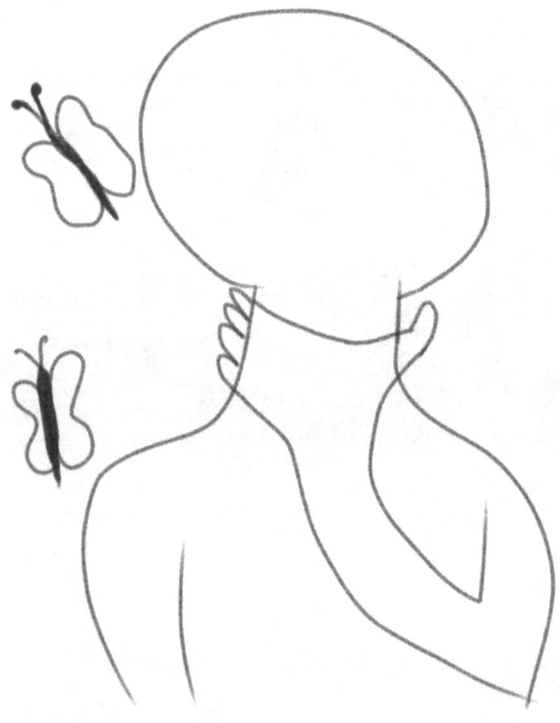

DEPARTURE
I still can't
make peace
with your departure.

DETACHED SOULS

When we detached
I had no clue
I might end up
regretting the
distance so hard.

CRAZY IN LOVE
Its crazy
how in love we
become submissive
to each other and
end up emptying ourselves.

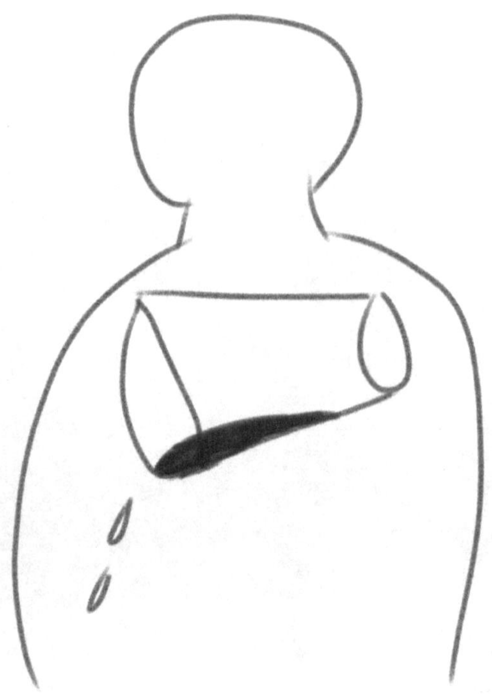

FADING PAIN

The pain's gonna fade away and
The wounds would heal with time.
I can't let it ruin my heart
and laugh is a shield i use to
protect it, only used when i
am craving tears.
I don't confining in people
only roar alone.
"Pain's gonna fade away
wounds will heal with time. "

STORIES WITHIN

We are all stories

Stories buried beneath our skin

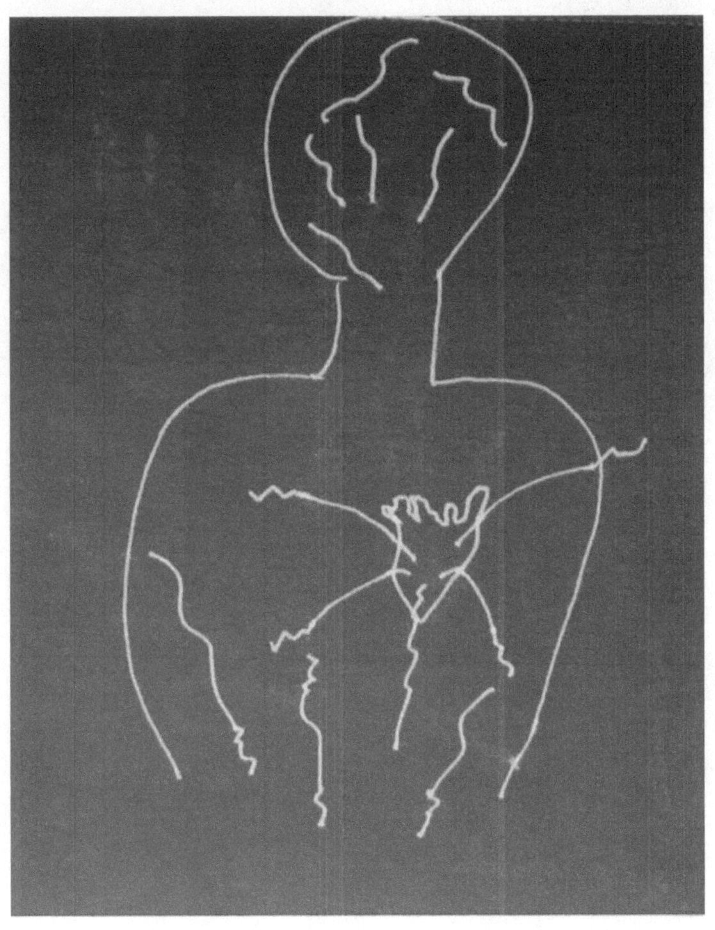

WILTING

WILTING
Our backs have not known
composure since ages
and we are made to wilt,
rot and subsume.

BURY MY SINS
And after you
I don't handle my sins
I bury them in to people

OH ! MY LOVE
Oh tell me
My love
When did you buried me
When did you arrange my farewell
And how could you not invite me to that
Oh tell me my love
When did we overcome each other
When did we grow so much
That we faced of fear of Losing us
Why didnt you cry when I die
I die every moment , every mini second
Without you , around
And time has done the other part
You don't miss me anymore
Do you ?

OH ! MY LOVE
Oh tell me
My love
When did you found someone
more safe than me
And like a FLOWER losing its softness
Losing its fragrance
With every passing day
I am dried out , my cries don't scream anymore
But I am sure , you really don't miss me anymore .
Do you ?
Tell me
my love .

SHE
And this time.
When she walked out of the room
I knew
She is in New hunt
She , again
Feel the need
Of blood
Of wounds
And the frailed bodies
Beware you selfless people
She ll cut you off
With her
Love
Do Bluff that looks real
In case you didn't know
I warn you
She is outside , maybe knocking your door
Trying to reduce you
Looking like a lady but
She is ready for perfect crime
Dreams look alike her
Making your favourite food
Pancakes on the floor
And you alive and naked yet baked
For her dine .
She is on her hunt

And this time.
When she walked out of the room
I knew she's sandra in love with her booze
- Bukowski' tales

WIPE OUT

Nothing in this world

Can rescue you

Except Yourself

- wipe out

VICTIM & CRIMINALS

The victim get hurt one time

But criminals

they are wrecked two times .

One , when people hurt them

And don't realise

Never come back and say sorry

Second , when they aim at their prey

They do the crime

And justify to save themselves

Their Soul

But they are a prey

Both people ,who play ,

victim And criminals who really once were innocent

- criminals who once were victim

HEART OF COURAGE
To take all the leftover pieces
And cry
Take a heart of courage .

SNAKES

If you ll keep on feeding the snakes

So that they don't hiss at you

my dear , your pet is going kill you soon .

- not even for hunger but for thirst of existence

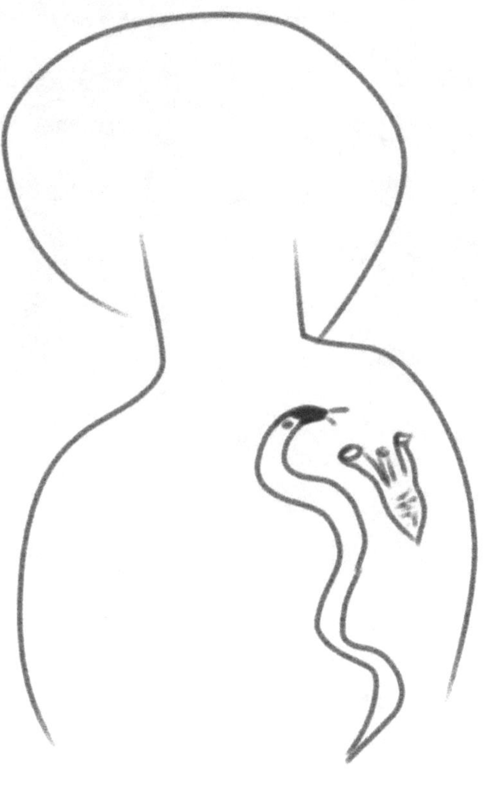

CRACKED SOUL

Don't let them know what cracks your soul.

- love that hurts so much in reciprocal .

SIMPLE THINGS

We often fail to see soul
in the most simplest things
like a smile from all heart
or a road full of trees
a fresh breeze of air
a kind hearted person
A child clinged to his mother
a walk under the moon
or a sky with twinkling stars
Things like these will stay in our memories forever
because our souls feel the beauty of such moments.
Nature 's embrace is the best place to feel
enriched with love
and the selfless care like mother's .
We often tend to get swayed
by the material things
that we forget our soul
is fed with love not with materiality.
Our souls don't run for food ,
they strive for attention ,
care and immense support.
At times when things outside fail
to appreciate the need of serenity
we shift to simplicity
thats small
yet the impact

is huge

ART
On the nights when you can't sleep
And your eyes are wailing
With No life around
I hope you find art
A strong sense of art

SINNER

Only god can accept you as your are
Only he can embrace your imperfactions
We are a pinch of what he is
Both extrems live in him
with him
and it does happen to people
whilst it should not
and in the end he conquers all
- A man is a natural sinner

YOU SEE THE OUTSIDE

You see the outside
Body, face, hands and waist
But grace is inside
Look within
Dive deep in it
that's when you ll find
the real me.
Do what's undone
Something not thought before
I would rather want to explored than told
I am a sea, of possibilities , imaginations and creations
Walk the pave to my heart
See the unseen yet
Talk like I have never heard before
That's when you know the real me
The soul inside this body,face , hands and waist
I am a world on my own
Let's roam back and forth
To experience unthinkables
I am me .. my type
Is rare
A human , a walking miracle
And a survivor
All in all
A someone always yearning for love, life and hope
And some light maybe..

You see the outside

Body, face, hands and waist

But grace is inside

Look within

Dive deep in it

TONGUE

Tongue is a sharpest sword
almost all of us own
use it when necessary.

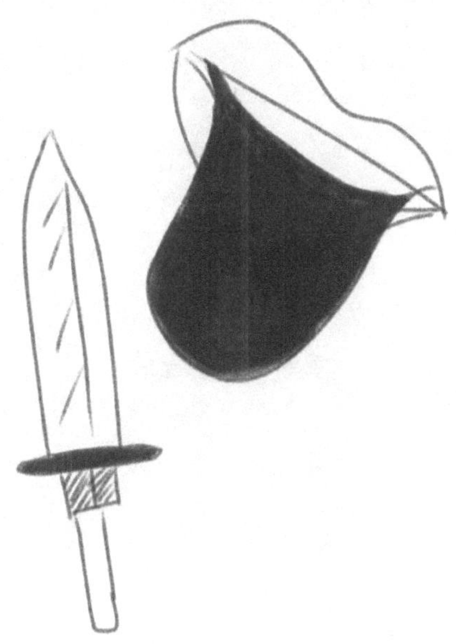

DON'T

I am nothing without art
Like humanity leaves my body
drenching my soul with pain , hurt and sadness
writing it down saves me
helps me stop the kill
God forbids why this world consumes creativity.
- Don't sour your tiny heart

SHRED OF SAND

Emotions make us human

We are a shred of sand otherwise

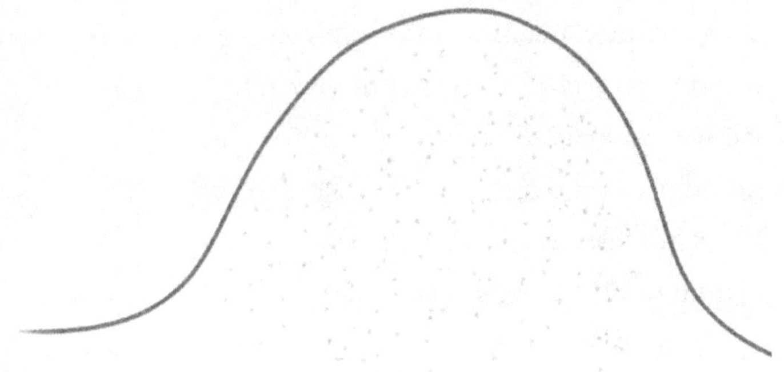

WARRIOR

and I don't see no warrior
I see a defeated man .. yes a someone
whose big dreams were squished in a confined box.
I look back and see myself as
I Ain't no James Bond,
just a common man shredded In pieces
juggling to carry all the sanity in my mind
and behave a certain way.
No I don't see no fighter , a survivor maybe
Like a homeless man standing
in front of his burned home,
trying to recall befores
and imagine the afters.
I look back
and I see
Honestly, A remainder harsh man
looking at the sky with an hopeless eye
and a lot of maybes could'ves what ifs ..
I look back and I realise
As people say we all have pain
in within ourselves
And With moving miseries
I learnt to live with it , in it
clearly forgotten about the other end of it..

SLOW POISON

When I was young they
told me love is butterflies
Later when I loved ,
i learnt Iove is sweet
Until it kills you
-slow poison

NEAR AND FAR

When I was near you
I never realised
I had to keep running
Away from you

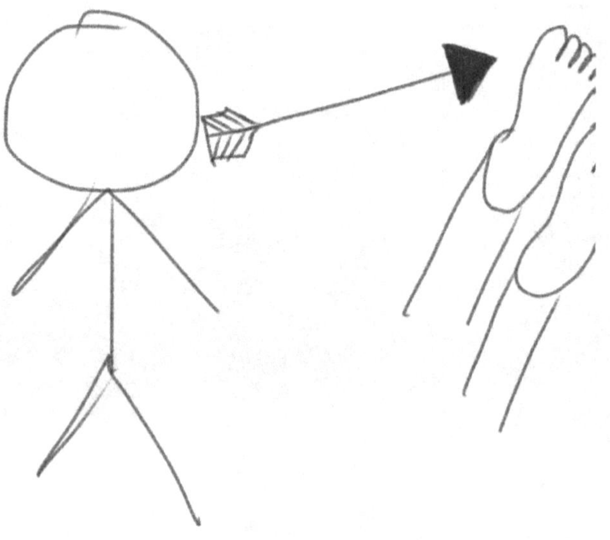

RISEN FROM ASHES

There are days when I let stress consume me

Slit open my mind and let anxiety come

out bursting through my throat

My shoulders feel coldness like a

shimmer of light force

opening my wings to fly

-Risen from the ashes

EAT IN PIECES
I will
Cut fat
Into pieces
And eat it.
-For Love

SNAKES & LADDERS

A man is the only living being
who can betray himself
-snakes and ladders

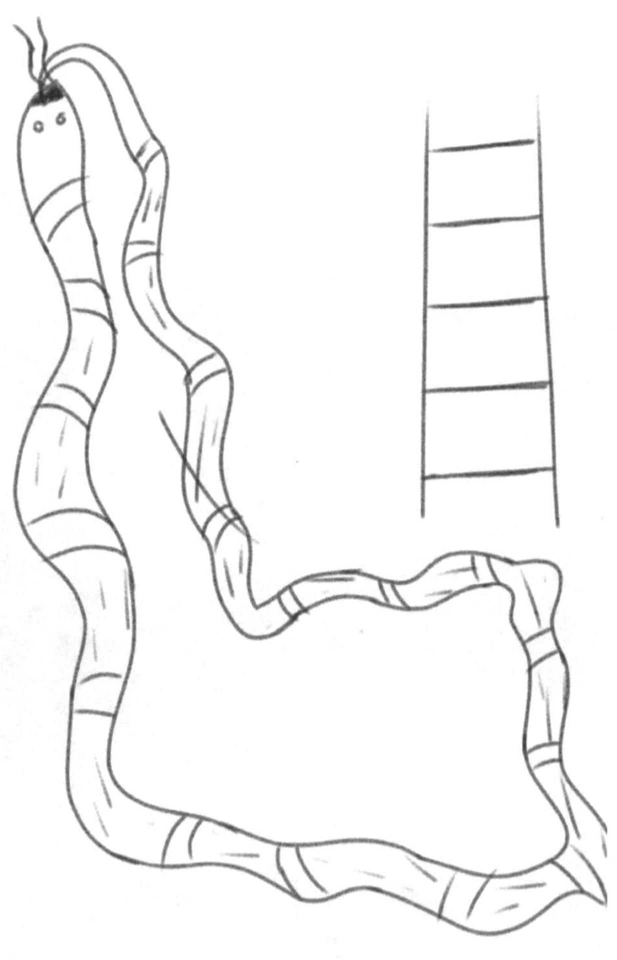

DEPRESSION

Depression is nothing
but suppressed
unheard, unsung
unknown emotions
As you continue to experience different emotions
you learn more about expression.
How important it is
for humans
to relate and communicate themselves.

WELCOME TO THE WALLS

I come back home
to the walls
And know how lonely
we both are
without you

DON'T TELL
NO ONE

A BUBBLE

What have Life made of me

I wonder

What

A bubble

Of fear

Love hate

And courage

Revenge

Or forgiveness

LOVe

SINCE YOU LEFT

It's been long since you left

And I am in denial

I am in agony

I am numb to feel emotions

It's been long since you left

And I still stumble to step ahead

Maybe because I forgot how to walk

How to move without having you beside me

HAPPINESS IS MANMADE

Home is a feeling

Person is an alternative

Emotions are to feel

Mind is for clarity

Soul is for peace

Happiness is man made

4. REVIVAL

REVIVAL

SEEDED BEAUTY

SEEDED BEAUTY

Beauty
was seeded
in our being
through nature
which is ever-evolving
in our conciousness.

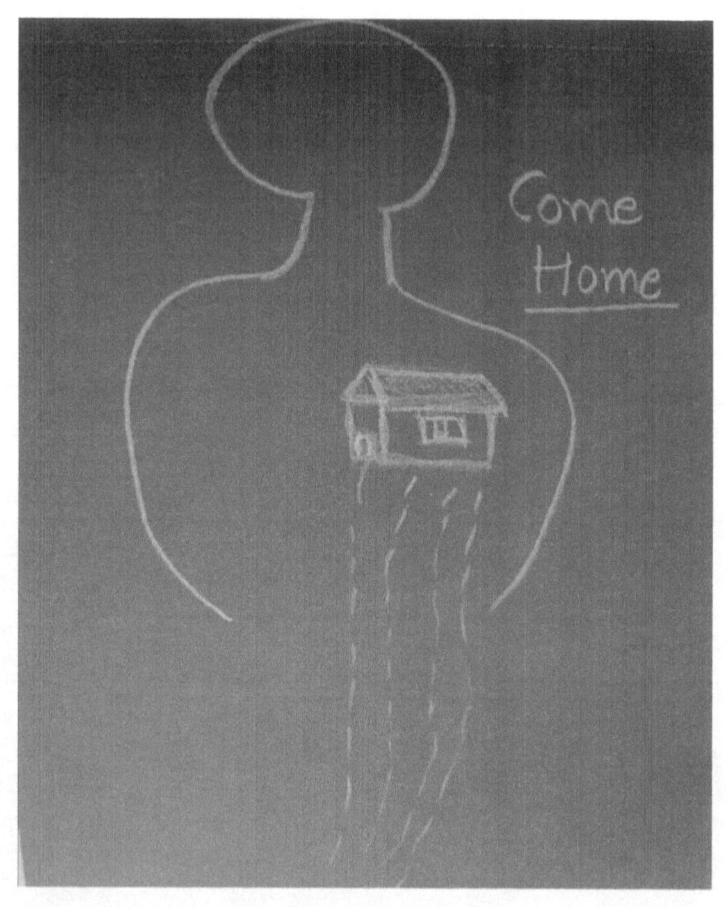

COME HOME

FLOWER

I haven't loved you like a flower
I have loved a bit more than that
A bit more tender
A bit more carefully
A bit more heartily
A bit more soulfully
A bit more a body heart mind and soul should
- I haven't loved you like a flower
I have loved a bit more than that

SECRET

Loving you is a
Secret
I am never going to
Reveal or maybe
I am so lucky
That for once
I knew love
Because of you.

TORE APART

Tore apart
Skin to skin
And pleasure
for the senses
that's how
I knew you.

IN BETWEEN

If sanity and I

have to walk

the same path over

It would be

Somewhere

In between.

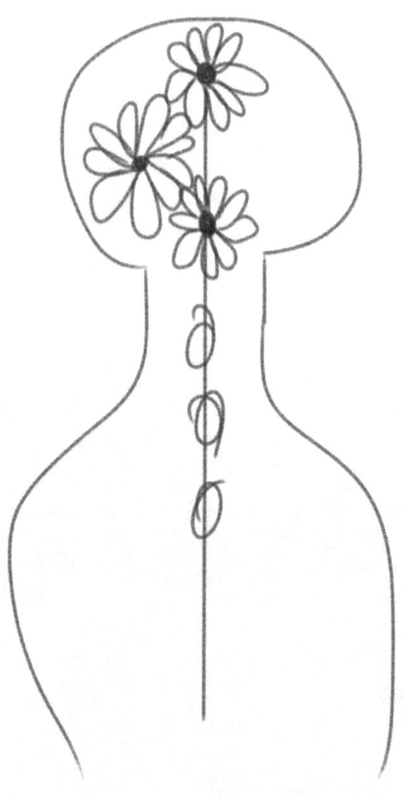

LUST
After a point,
I am thirsty
If you are skin
-Lust

DESTROY THE DELICACY

Don't be beautiful

And delicate

People destroy

Such things.

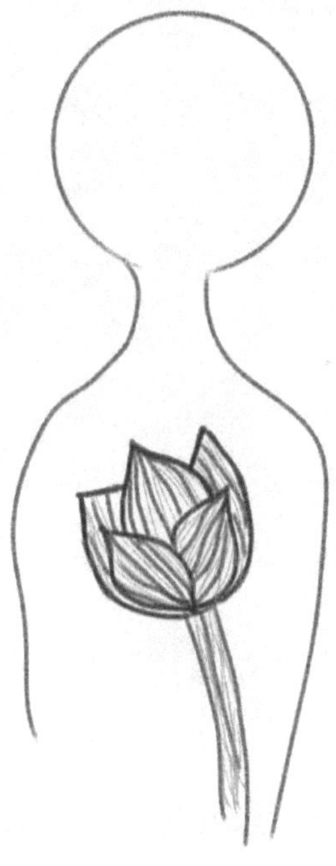

SURVIVAL
Only in the utter
survival people tend
to reveal their
trueselves.

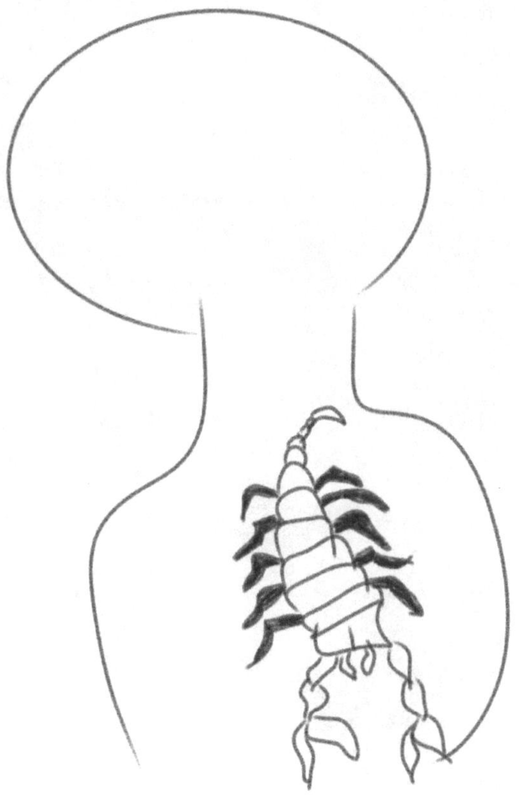

READ LOVE
You read
what I write
Its full of
longingness
and
despair.

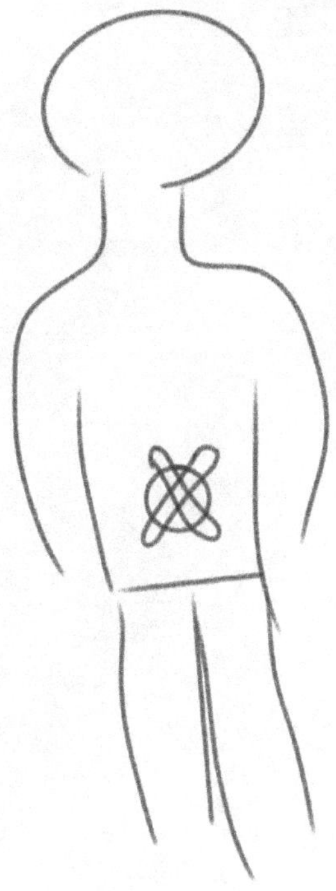

STAG OF SKIN

I am mere
Stag of skin
without you.

SEW THE HEART
People change
I see them changing
It hurts me
everytime
I had to sew that
part of my heart
reserved for them.

WE

We are strikingly alike

Like How poetry embellishes a blank paper

And sea shines better in nights

Like rain beautify thedry land

And the sun follows the moon.

PARALLEL UNIVERSE
And somewhere in the parallel universe
We sync perfectly
like lyrics of a
meodious song
The rhythm of our love chords
echoed blooming the whole galaxy.

SOIL

You are the soil

I plant

my emptiness in.

FEELING OF LOVE

You are that

Feeling of love

I have held

Strong

In my existence.

DEEPALI SEKHRI

EXPRESSION

I have started

To fumble

At words

I used to express

ENEMIES
If enemy
will unrest
My safe place
Its my duty
to undress
its witch will
to GOD.

SURRENDER

I surrender to your thougths
Like
Soul surrender to God.

FIRE
When I leave
The town
Turn me into fire
Of cremination
BUT
Don't fire me
With seperation.

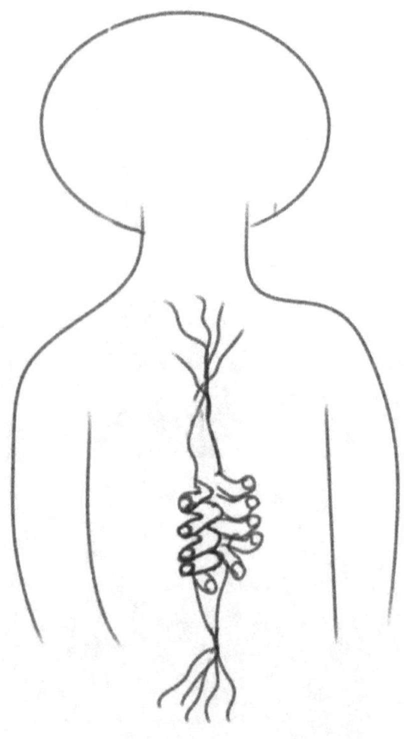

LURKING MIND

Our minds are like unhinged machines
And you continue to stimulate it
With feelings, emotions and connections.

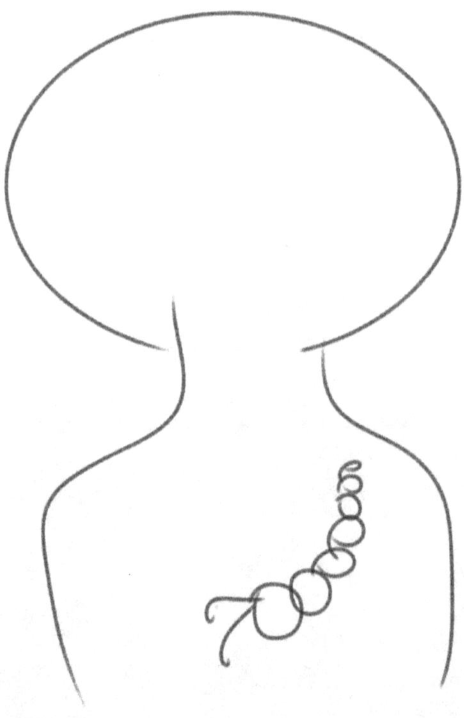

DEAD

Dead's don't return back.

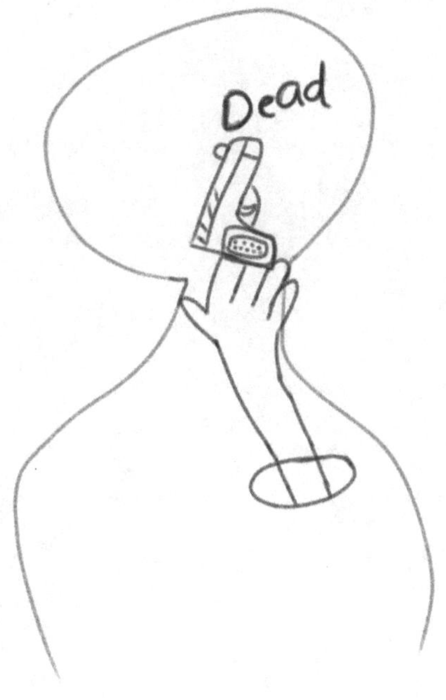

TEMPERED

Value the innocent
heart
before its
tampered.

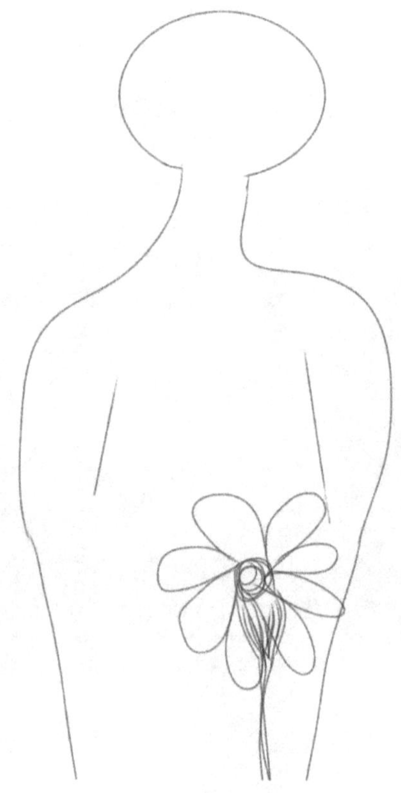

SADNESS

Sadness revolves around you

And you lose your sense of soul

And in the dark

Only selfishness exist

Only void

That you know

You can't refill'

It is existent.

-Hollow

THOUGHTS
Thoughts that I can't say
or emotions that I keep
hiding beneath
the layer of skin
all combined
are intrigued
by the idea
of you.

UNSEEN

If we struggle to meet

In tangible world

Lets meet in

Intangible world.

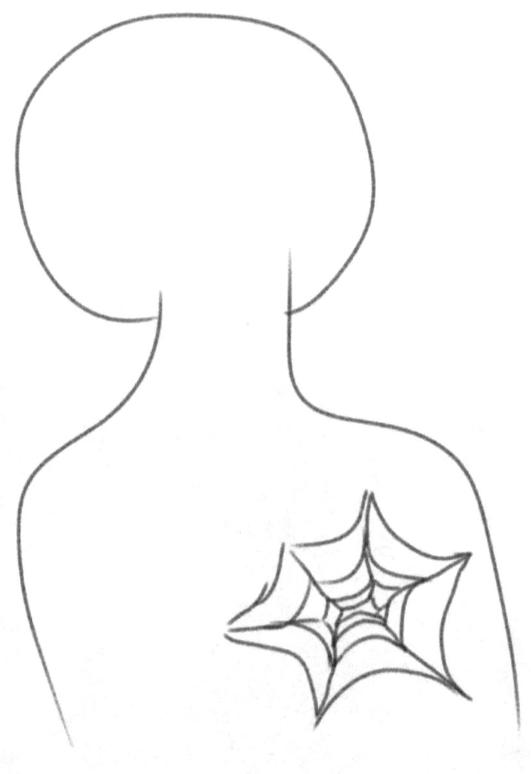

BREATHING

Some days it pains
So much
That breathing feels
Like burden.

SEEDS OF LOVE

DISAPPEAR
I had so many
Skins to wear
Given by you
Just when you
Were about to
Disappear into an
Unknown , untracable
World, with or without
Reasonings.

DIFFICULT DAYS

Difficult days teach you to spread love to people the way you love yourself despite the changes, the breakouts. That People fail miserably, they fall down and try their best to come out strongly. Diificult days teach life never stays consitent. It fluctuates like feelings in humans. We need to keep loving people despite their flaws, their failures, their winning or any other thing that matters to us. Difficult days teach you to be humble, respectful and calm even in the most chaotic situations. Not everyday we can shoot a star, it's a way how GOD makes us more of a human than a fucking warrior who only knows how to cut and kneel down.

REFLECTION OF LIFE
what your departure cost me
life dtripping out of my body
in drops
and a continuous thrist I feel
without needing water.
Your reflection flows me
like a shadow
and the nights
are becoming scarier.
You absence is a slow poison to me ,
the more I realise that you are gone,
the more its killing me inside.

Like a lifeless soul
whenever I breathe
it feels like a needle
causing severe ache.
Your absence sounds
like a curse to me.
what your departure cost me

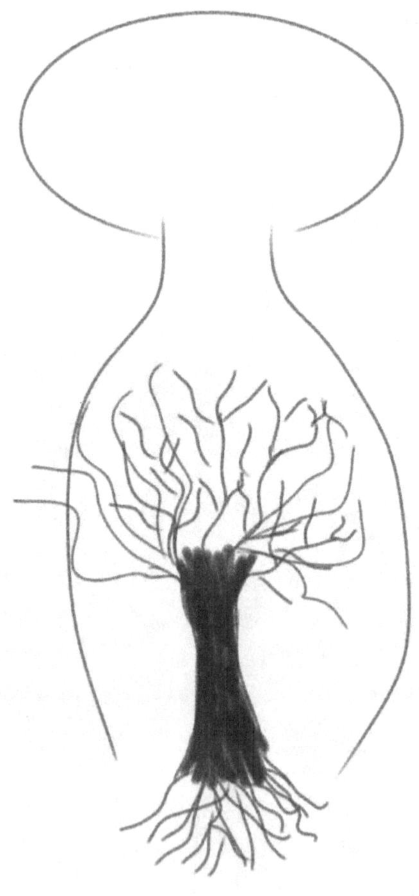

MERMAID

I am something more
Something more than your normal thought
My uniqueness defines my maker
I am the holder, the elegance
I am the differentiation from this uniform world
Undoubtedly I am made yet a mermaid
I am the spirit that drives your soul
The sensation running through your beating heart
I am the sparkle that makes you shine
I am a poem that a writer wants to write every night
I am the divineness , you move to find in the shrine
I am the hope of a shining morning light
I am the story your crave to read
Yes, I am in prayer, I am the healer
I am the creation of the supreme creator.

MERMAID

WITHERING

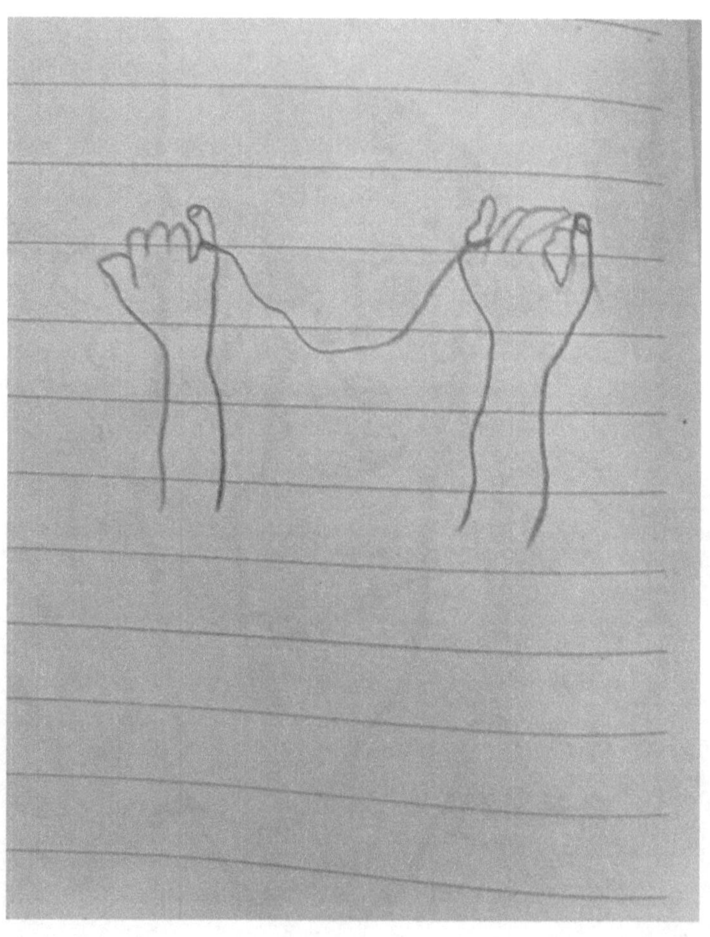

CONNECTED

Connect On

instagram handle : deepali_sekhri11
youtube: youtube.com/deepalisekhri11

About The Author

Deepali Sekhri is an Indian author. "Scars on the soul" is her first published book . She is a poet and illustrator. She is a qualified Company Secretary with postgrad in Commerce. She writes about pain, love, grief, hopefulness and soul journey. This book is a poet's journey , courage, power and resilience being formed as a part of book in words or illustrations. This book is collection of soul captivating verses. The book will walk you through edge of life , medieval human journey , inevitable regrets and everchanging process of healing, peace and truthfulness of soul in darkness. It will bind you together while addressing your scattered pieces. The book is the celebration of hope and relentless to quit when you are thrown in dark. Her words are reflection of her believe in light, life and love.

www.ingramcontent.com/pod-product-compliance
Lightning Source LLC
Chambersburg PA
CBHW020334180726
47991CB00020B/1626